Religion and Free Speech Today
A Pro/Con Debate

ISSUES IN FOCUS TODAY

Joan Vos MacDonald

Enslow Publishers, Inc.
40 Industrial Road
Box 398
Berkeley Heights, NJ 07922
USA

http://www.enslow.com

Library of Congress Cataloging-in-Publication Data

MacDonald, Joan Vos.
  Religion and free speech today : a pro/con debate / Joan Vos MacDonald.
    p. cm.—(Issues in focus today)
  Summary: "Discusses religious issues and the freedom of speech in the United States today, including the separation of church and state and the debate over prayer and religious displays in public schools"—Provided by publisher.
  Includes bibliographical references and index.
  ISBN-13: 978-0-7660-2915-6
  ISBN-10: 0-7660-2915-8
  1. Church and state--United States—Juvenile literature. 2. Freedom of religion—United States—Juvenile literature. I. Title. II. Series.
  KF4865.Z9M33 2009
  342.7308'52—dc22
                                        2007045766

Printed in the United States of America

10 9 8 7 6 5 4 3 2 1

To Our Readers: We have done our best to make sure all Internet addresses in this book were active and appropriate when we went to press. However, the author and the publisher have no control over and assume no liability for the material available on those Internet sites or on other Web sites they may link to. Any comments or suggestions can be sent by e-mail to comments@enslow.com or to the address on the back cover.

♻ Enslow Publishers, Inc., is committed to printing our books on recycled paper. The paper in every book contains 10% to 30% post-consumer waste (PCW). The cover board on the outside of each book contains 100% PCW. Our goal is to do our part to help young people and the environment too!

Illustration Credits: AP/Wide World, pp. 8, 30, 36, 40, 50 (top left, bottom right), 56, 77, 82, 84, 97, 105; The Image Works, pp. 3, 13, 35, 50 (top right), 66; iStockphoto.com, pp. 50 (bottom left), 52, 103; Library of Congress, pp. 3, 17, 20, 43, 71, 95, 99; Shutterstock, pp. 1, 3, 5, 27, 47, 59, 74, 79, 87, 93, 101.

Cover Illustration: Shutterstock (large photo); BananaStock (small inset photo).

Contents

Religion and Public Life

1

In 1999, Nick Becker, a senior in a Calvert County, Maryland, high school, decided to stand up for his rights. First, he refused to rise for the Pledge of Allegiance during a high school assembly. Later, he protested the prayer high school officials planned for his graduation ceremony.

When the Northern High School senior refused to stand up for the pledge, school officials threatened to suspend him. Becker contacted the American Civil Liberties Union (ACLU), an organization that defends the free-speech rights Americans are guaranteed by the U.S. Constitution.[1]

Lawyers at the ACLU informed his school that according to

the law of the land, Becker could not be made to stand for the pledge. Nor could any other student. This had been decided in a Supreme Court case known as *West Virginia Board of Education* v. *Barnette*, 1943.[2]

When he heard that a fellow student would recite a prayer at his class's upcoming graduation ceremony, Becker protested. He knew that student-led prayer at graduation ceremonies had been declared unconstitutional by the Supreme Court in a 1992 case known as *Lee* v. *Weisman*. That means the Supreme Court decided such prayers did not follow the intention of the Constitution, the law of the land.[3]

In response to his protests, an official prayer was dropped from the graduation agenda. A moment of silence would take its place.

At the ceremony, during the moment of silence, audience members started to recite a well-known Christian prayer. Becker walked out in protest. When the prayer was over, he tried to reenter the ceremony to get his diploma. The police stopped him and threatened to arrest him. As a result, he missed his own high school graduation.

Becker, who does not see himself as an atheist, says he is merely trying to figure things out—but he feels strongly that schools should not impose religious practices on anyone. He says this is a right granted to everyone by the First Amendment to the U.S. Constitution.

Was Becker a hero defending his First Amendment rights under the U.S. Constitution? Or was he an atheist who wanted to deny others the chance to freely express their religious beliefs? That depends on your point of view. Both these descriptions reflect different points of view expressed about the eighteen-year-old student.

The First Amendment

The First Amendment to the U.S. Constitution states:

> Congress shall make no law respecting an establishment of religion, or prohibiting the free exercise thereof; or abridging the freedom of speech, or of the press; or the right of the people peaceably to assemble, and to petition the Government for a redress of grievances.

The First Amendment has two parts: The Establishment Clause and the Free Exercise Clause. The Establishment Clause says the government cannot favor any religion, and the Free Exercise Clause says people have a right to freely worship.

While some people might think Becker defended his rights under the Establishment Clause, others think he challenged the Free Exercise Clause—the right of Americans to freely worship and express their religious beliefs. For that, some people said, he deserved to be shut out at his own graduation.[4]

Do Religious Students Have Rights?

While Becker objected to expressions of religion in school, other students have taken a stand against school regulations that they feel deny them a fair chance to express their faith. One example of a student who fought to express her faith at school is Tausha Prince, an eleventh grader at Spanaway Lake High School in Washington State. Prince wanted to form a Christian Bible Club, but her school denied the group financial support and access to the school's public-address system.

Prince felt that the school district violated her First Amendment rights to freely express her religion—and that her club was being discriminated against.[5] Prince took her case to court, where it was known as *Prince* v. *Jacoby*. Judge Kim M. Wardlaw of U.S. Ninth Circuit Court of Appeals ruled that Bible clubs should be treated like any other extracurricular activity, which means schools must provide access to space and supplies. After the ruling, the club was allowed to use school equipment and employ school buses for field trips. According to a law known as the Equal Access Act of 1984, such supplies cannot be denied just because a club is religious.[6]

When the court ruled in her favor, Prince was pleased. "It took a long time, but it was worth the wait," she said.[7]

Interpreting the First Amendment

Both Nick Becker and Tausha Prince felt that their First Amendment rights had been denied even though they disagreed on what rôle religion should play in the public school system— or other parts of public life. These students' stories illustrate how complicated the debate about religion in public life can be.

Defying a court order, students recite the Lord's Prayer at a graduation ceremony in Russell Springs, Kentucky, in 2006. Such publicly sponsored prayers were found unconstitutional by the Supreme Court in 1992.

During the last fifty years, such debate has centered around whether schools can lead prayers, whether the words *under God* belong in the Pledge of Allegiance, whether the Ten Commandments should be displayed in public courthouses, and how religious holidays should be celebrated in public spaces. Rulings in court cases have often confused people, and attempts to follow them have further complicated the issues.

Many people feel that court rulings on these subjects do not reflect the opinions of the majority and that the Founding Fathers never meant for the government to be completely religion-free. They just meant for it not to favor any one religion. Others don't think the rulings go far enough in separating the government and religion.

Has Christmas Been Stolen?

Christmas has been described as a holiday of "peace and goodwill" but misunderstandings about how this holiday should be celebrated in public life have caused many arguments.

For example, in the Jackson County School System in Georgia, teachers received the following guidelines: Nativity scenes could not be set up in class and teachers could not wish students "Merry Christmas." Teachers could not wear holiday pins, angels, crosses, or clothing with religious connotations.

The school district did not want to seem to endorse any one religion's celebrations. They asked teachers and staff members to be sensitive to the fact that students who do not celebrate Christmas might feel left out.

However, one teacher at an after-school program in the district's Benton Elementary School felt such restrictions violated the rights of those who did celebrate Christmas. That teacher said the guidelines kept Christians from expressing their religious views and asked the Alliance Defense Fund (ADF), a legal defense group that works on religious freedom cases, to write to the school district.

"Frankly, it's ridiculous that we're even discussing whether it's okay to say 'Merry Christmas,'" said David Cortman, a lawyer representing ADF. "I'm sure just about everyone would rather have a merry Christmas than a meaningless winter holiday."[8]

But would they? Or could such wishes and public displays of celebrations make people with different beliefs feel as if they were forced into celebrating a holiday they did not observe? Does saying "Merry Christmas" in school violate the separation of church and state written in the First Amendment, or does being forbidden to say "Merry Christmas" violate the right to freely express your religious beliefs?

Separation of Church and State

Religion has been a topic of debate since North America was first settled. Many of the nation's first settlers came to North America because they were fleeing religious persecution. Once they arrived, many set about creating colonies with official religions. For example, the Puritans came to the colonies looking for a safe place to practice their faith, yet they were surprisingly intolerant of anyone who disagreed with their beliefs.

The Founding Fathers added an amendment to the Constitution separating church and state and requiring religious freedom. They did so because they had seen the damage done by government-endorsed churches in Europe and the conflicts already being caused by religion within the colonies. Several of the colonies collected a tax to support their official churches and discriminated against people who were not of the majority religion.

Since the First Amendment was added to the Constitution, it has been examined in many court cases. Some say the laws have been reinterpreted to reflect changing times and values; others say that the courts have misunderstood what the Founding Fathers originally intended.

A Nativity Scene and a Menorah

Organizations that describe themselves as conservative, such as the Alliance Defense Fund (ADF), say that liberals are trying to do away with the nation's religious heritage and traditions—and organizations such as the American Civil Liberties Union (ACLU) are helping them.

The ACLU, whose lawyers have opposed ADF lawyers in court cases, says they are trying to protect the nation's heritage by keeping religion and government separate, so that people of all faiths—and no faith—have equal rights.

During the past few decades, the ACLU has supplied legal help in several cases about religious displays in government buildings. One recent court case in Cranston, Rhode Island, centered on a holiday display on city government grounds. The display included a life-size nativity scene and a menorah.[9]

"I feel very strongly that religion simply is not the business of government," said Grace C. Osediacz, a city resident who began the suit. "Rhode Island was founded on the principle that religion and government should be separate. I'm outraged that any public official would invite the placement of religious symbols right in front of City Hall."[10]

Osadiacz lost her case when a federal judge ruled that the city could have private religious holiday displays on its lawn. The ADF proclaimed this a victory.

"The ACLU long ago decided it wanted to be Uncle Scrooge and expend its energies saying 'bah humbug' to public Christmas displays, but they are out of touch with the 96 percent of Americans that celebrate Christmas," said Gary McCaleb, ADF senior counsel.[11]

The ACLU says they are not Scrooge. Nor are they "The Grinch Who Stole Christmas." They say they are merely trying to make sure one religion is not disproportionately represented in holiday displays and they will defend anyone who feels his or her First Amendment rights are threatened by such displays.

In its summer 1999 Briefing Paper entitled "Church and State," the ACLU said:

> Commitment to the separation of church and state is not an anti-religion stance. Indeed, it is the best guarantee that each individual has the right to practice his or her religion, without coercion, hostility or violence. Keeping religion out of the hands of the government is our best guarantee for continued religious freedom and religious harmony.[12]

According to the ACLU, there are several things to consider when deciding how appropriate holiday displays on public property are. For instance, any displays that promote religion are probably not okay. If some religious displays are included in a nonreligious display, then it's probably acceptable. A nativity scene or menorah by itself would not be okay. However, a nativity scene surrounded by plastic reindeer and a Santa Claus, or a menorah next to a Christmas tree, would be appropriate. If the overall message is one of cultural diversity or a general celebration of the winter holidays, then it's probably constitutional.

Holiday Celebrations and Free Speech

These distinctions can be confusing. Finding ways to recognize religion in public life without promoting one religion over another has been a challenge for parents, schools, and public officials.

Lisa Lowry of Scarborough, Maine, was annoyed when her children were told they might offend fellow classmates by wishing them a "Merry Christmas." But when she learned that the December band concert that her daughter was playing in would include Hanukkah and winter songs—but no Christmas music—Lowry decided her daughter's middle school was trying too hard to be politically correct. A fellow parent, Doreen Duval-Flaherty, agreed. "For me, it is not about religion," she said. "It's a free speech and fairness issue. If you live in fear of offending the kid sitting next to you, you will never get to know them or understand them and you won't be able to celebrate their culture as well as yours."[13]

The parents spoke to school administrators and the school came up with a plan. A rabbi and a minister were invited to an assembly about the holidays. Children now read about Hanukkah and Kwanzaa as well as Christmas, and school decorations include Christmas trees, a menorah, and Kwanzaa symbols.[14]

Wearing Your Faith

Would you be willing to be suspended from school for wearing a symbol of your faith? That's what happened to Nashala Hearn, a sixth grader at the Benjamin Franklin Science Academy in Muskogee, Oklahoma.[15] Hearn, who is Muslim,

Middle schoolers play in a holiday concert. Controversy has arisen over which holidays should be celebrated as part of school activities.

decided to wear a head scarf known as a hijab, which is an expression of faith and culture for many Muslim women.

At first, the school's reaction was positive. But around the second anniversary of the September 11 attacks on the World Trade Center and the Pentagon by Middle Eastern terrorists, however, the school decided that her hijab looked too much like a bandanna, which the school dress code banned in an effort to curb gang violence. (The dress code also banned hats, caps, and jacket hoods.)[16] Hearn was suspended, refused to take off her head scarf, came back to school, and was suspended again.

After Hearn was suspended, her family took the school to court. They won their case, and the school dress code must now make exceptions for religious attire.

"Public schools cannot require students to check their faith at the school house door," said R. Alexander Acosta, assistant district attorney general for civil rights at the Department of Justice. "The Department of Justice will not tolerate discrimination against Muslims or any other religious group."[17]

Hearn says the experience has taught her an important lesson about her rights to free expression.[18]

Legal Heritage or Religious Display?

Most people would agree that religious values have helped shape the nation's laws. However, courts have ruled that displaying them may be closer to making a religious statement than a historical one.

The Ten Commandments are laws that Jews, Christians, and Muslims believe were given to Moses by God. There are three different versions in the Hebrew Scriptures. Protestants and Catholics also use different versions. Yet a different phrasing and order of the Ten Commandments is included in the Qur'an.

During the 1950s and 1960s, as many as four thousand statues and monuments with one version of the Ten

Commandments were set up in public parks and public buildings by the Fraternal Order of Eagles, a public service group. But in the last few years, court cases have challenged whether it is constitutional for a religious text to be displayed in a government building or on government property.[19]

Those who argue in favor of displaying the Ten Commandments say they helped shape the nation's laws. Those opposed to displaying the Ten Commandments say that the government should not endorse religion because the Ten Commandments belong only to a few religions, and the version found on public monuments is a Protestant version. If you are going to pick a version, whose version should you choose—and who will feel left out, if you don't choose his or her version?

In April 2002, a federal judge in Pennsylvania ordered the removal of an eighty-two-year-old Ten Commandments plaque from the Chester County Courthouse in Philadelphia, calling it unconstitutional. This version of the Ten Commandments was derived from the King James Bible used by Protestants.

"The tablet's necessary effect on those who see it is to endorse or advance the unique importance of this predominantly religious text for mainline Protestantism," said U.S. District Judge Stewart Dalzell.[20]

In Ogden, Utah, a similar Ten Commandments plaque was removed because a religious group felt that a public space or "public forum" should provide an equal opportunity to share their message.

In 1994, a religious group known as Summum, which believes in ancient Egyptian practices, such as mummification, asked the town to display their Principles of Summum next to the Ten Commandments on the courthouse lawn.[21] Town residents refused, saying the Ten Commandments were significant in the history of the United States, whereas the Summum principles were not. The Summum group said their right to freely express their religion was being denied.

In 2002, the U.S. Court of Appeals ruled that "Summum's amended complaint sufficiently alleges that a limited public forum has been created and that the County engaged in viewpoint discrimination in violation of Summum's free speech rights."[22] This meant that as long as the Ten Commandments were displayed in this public space, any other religious group could also display its principles. Rather than permit the addition of the Summum display, the town removed the Ten Commandments.[23]

Protesting a Monument

In Frederick, Maryland, an Urbana High School student, Blake Trettien, eighteen, wrote to his city council about a Ten Commandments monument that had been standing in a city park for forty-four years. He said that federal courts in other jurisdictions had ruled that identical monuments violated the Constitution.[24] "Our civil liberties and the separation of church and state have been very important to me, and have always interested me," said Trettien.[25]

When the city refused to remove the monument, Trettien called the ACLU. His story was written up in several newspapers, with one editorial referring to him as "the snot-nosed kid." "Another told me to simply keep my mouth shut and learn something," said Trettien. "It's obvious, they said, Frederick County is a Christian county." In the end, the issue was resolved when the town sold the monument—and the land it was on—to a private party.[26]

The debate about the place of religion in public life continues and continues to inspire new court cases. Rulings by the Supreme Court have established some guidelines. Studying the history of the debate can help readers learn more about its past and draw their own conclusions.

At the time of the colonization of America, many European countries had official religions. People who wanted to worship in a different way were persecuted. Most of the early colonists who crossed the ocean to settle in North America wanted to practice their own faith without persecution.

Europe in the Sixteenth Century

Many of the New World settlers were Protestant. The Protestant movement began in 1517, when a monk named Martin Luther demanded that the Catholic Church be reformed and return to what he considered a simpler, truer form of Christianity. This led to the formation of several Protestant religious groups, including the Calvinist, Lutheran, and Anabaptist.

Religious differences in the sixteenth century led to wars and executions. The Inquisition, an investigation launched by the Catholic Church in the late fifteenth century, sought to convert or execute nonbelievers throughout Europe. In Spain, many Jews who did not want to convert were killed or had to leave the country. Many synagogues were burned.

In 1534, England's King Henry VIII established a new church so he could divorce his first wife. The Catholic Church did not permit divorce. The nation's official religion became Anglican, but many Catholics continued to practice in secret. When his daughter Mary became queen and restored Catholicism as the national religion, so many Anglicans were killed that she became known as "Bloody Mary."[1] When Mary's half sister, Elizabeth I, became queen, she passed an act known as the Elizabethan Settlement, which again made the Anglican Church the official religion. The act said that people could believe what they wanted but could only practice the official faith.[2]

Most of the early colonists who crossed the ocean to settle in North America wanted to practice their own faith without persecution.

For many English subjects, this was not enough. Those seeking more religious freedom fled their native lands to live among strangers, often having to learn a new language and adopt new customs. That is what happened to the Puritans, an offshoot of the Reformed, or Calvinist, movement. The Puritans moved to the Netherlands, a country known for its religious tolerance, but they eventually established a colony of their own in Massachusetts.

Early Colonies

Once the Puritans settled in Massachusetts, their desire to preserve their own way of life made them as intolerant of other beliefs as the people who persecuted them. The Puritans punished, exiled, and even hanged people with differing beliefs. Anne Hutchinson, a Puritan who believed that women should be able to preach, was banished from the Massachusetts Bay colony. Mary Dyer, a member of the Society of Friends, known as Quakers, was banished; later when she tried to return to the colony, she was hanged.[3]

Many early colonies centered around one faith, and a few even had official religions. In Virginia, it was a crime not to have children baptized in the Anglican Church; not doing so could result in one's children being taken away. If you were a Christian and said you did not believe everything in the Bible, you could not hold office or join the military.[4]

A few colonies practiced tolerance and embraced religious diversity. Notable among them were Pennsylvania, founded by William Penn, a Quaker; Rhode Island, founded by Roger Williams, a Puritan exile; and Maryland, a primarily Catholic colony, which passed the Toleration Act of 1649, providing religious freedom—but only for Christians.[5]

Williams wanted to found a colony where there would be a "hedge or wall of separation between the garden of the church and the wilderness of the world." As governor of the colony, he welcomed people of all faiths, saying, "I commend that man, whether Jew, or Turk, or Papist, or whoever, that steers no otherwise than his conscience dares."[6]

What Did the Founding Fathers Mean?

While all of the authors of the Constitution came from Christian backgrounds and many attended church at least occasionally, the framers decided that the best way to create a strong government was to keep religion and government separate.

The religious views of many of the founders—Thomas Jefferson, John Adams, Benjamin Franklin, and James Madison—were influenced by a popular religious philosophy of the day known as Deism. Deists believed that religion was a personal matter between a man and his creator. Deists did not feel the need for regular attendance at any particular church.[7]

Some delegates to the Constitutional Convention argued for the formal recognition of Christianity in the Constitution. They said such language was necessary to "hold out some distinction between the professors of Christianity and downright infidelity or paganism." That view was not adopted.[8] The founding fathers decided that the best way to respect religion was to grant all religions equal rights and keep the nation free of religious strife.

Thomas Jefferson

Thomas Jefferson, author of the Declaration of Independence, sometimes attended a Unitarian church, which did not share the same beliefs as many other Christian denominations of the time. Writing to a Unitarian minister, he said: "I rejoice in this country of free inquiry and belief, which has surrendered its creed and conscience to neither kings nor priests."[9]

In a letter to the Danbury Baptist Association in the state of Connecticut, he declared that the government should "make no law respecting an establishment of religion, or

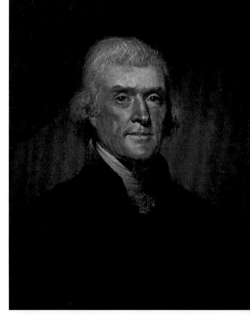

Thomas Jefferson was the author of the phrase "a wall of separation between church and state."

prohibiting the free exercise thereof, thus building a wall of Separation between church and state."[10]

Jefferson and James Madison worked together to create The Virginia Statute for Religious Freedom, a bill written by Jefferson in 1777 and proposed to the Virginia Legislature in 1779. In this bill, Jefferson said:

> Be it enacted by the General Assembly, That no man shall be compelled to frequent or support any religious worship, place, or ministry whatsoever, nor shall be enforced, restrained, molested, or [burdened] in his body or goods, nor shall otherwise suffer on account of his religious opinions or belief; but that all men shall be free to profess, and by argument to maintain, their opinion in matters of religion, and that the same shall in no wise diminish, enlarge, or affect their civil capacities.[11]

That meant that not only could people not be forced to worship, but they could express their religious beliefs, and those beliefs could not be held against them when they ran for office.

Religion and the Constitution

Delegates from the colonies met in Philadelphia in 1787 to write a national constitution and create a strong central government. They came to three conclusions on religious topics:

- No religious test or oath would be required for any federally elected office, which had been the case in some colonies.
- Quakers could state rather than swear their oaths of office, since swearing was not permitted in their religion.
- Christianity was not recognized as the nation's official religion. In fact, the nation was to have no official religion.[12]

These statements did not end all debate on religious freedom. Jefferson and Madison were among many of the founders who decided that the Constitution needed a more clearly detailed bill of rights.

Madison, who became known as the Father of the

Constitution, had witnessed a form of religious persecution when he was young. He saw Baptist ministers repeatedly jailed for preaching without permission from the state of Virginia. These incidents inspired his interest in religious liberty.[13] Madison thought the Constitution should include something similar to what Jefferson had written in the Virginia bill. He said it was important to state citizens' rights clearly, because "in all cases where a majority are united by a common interest or passion, the rights of the minority are in danger. What motives are to restrain them? Religion itself may become a motive to persecution and oppression."[14]

The First Amendment

In 1789, Madison introduced the first amendment to the Constitution, the first of the ten amendments known as the Bill of Rights. The bill was ratified by the states on December 15, 1791.

The part of the First Amendment that says the nation cannot establish a religion is known as the Establishment Clause. The part known as the Free Exercise Clause guarantees people the right to worship freely, whatever their religion.

The Treaty of Tripoli

One document that many people refer to when they dispute any notion that the United States is a Christian nation is the treaty of Tripoli, signed in 1797. The treaty was signed to assure safe passage of American ships in the Mediterranean shipping lanes, since these ships were no longer under British protection. As part of the treaty, money was paid to the Muslim sultan of Tripoli. The treaty says:

> As the government of the United States of America is not in any sense founded on the Christian Religion—as it has itself no character of enmity against the laws, religion or tranquility of Musselman—and as the said States have never entered into any war

or act of hostility against any Mehomitan nation, it is declared by the parties that no pretext arising from religious opinions shall ever produce an interruption of the harmony existing between the two countries.[15]

(*Musselman* and *Mehomitan* were terms used at the time to describe Muslims, or followers of Islam, and its prophet, Muhammad.)

The Fourteenth Amendment

Originally, the First Amendment applied only to the federal government, and states continued to make their own laws, which often favored specific religions. Some states had laws that only Christian ministers could perform marriages. Some states had laws saying people of a certain religion could not run for office. Other states gave financial support to particular churches. Such laws received more federal attention after 1868 with the passage of the Fourteenth Amendment.

The Fourteenth Amendment says:

No State shall make or enforce any law which shall abridge the privileges or immunities of citizens of the United States; nor shall any State deprive any person of life, liberty, or property, without due process of law; nor deny to any person within its jurisdiction the equal protection of the laws.

Although originally intended to put an end to slavery in Southern states at the end of the Civil War, the amendment was further used to enforce all the laws established in the Constitution.

Religious Expression Can Be Criminal

One of the first cases to arise out of the passage of the Fourteenth Amendment was *Reynolds* v. *U.S.* in 1879. In this case, a man named George Reynolds was arrested for marrying more than one wife. Reynolds was a member of The Church of

Jesus Christ of Latter-Day Saints, commonly known as Mormons, and he lived in the largely Mormon territory of Utah. At that time, the church's teachings included polygamy—the practice of marrying many wives.

The Supreme Court declared that a religious practice could only be permitted if it was not a civil crime, and polygamy was against the law. The federal government threatened to deny Utah the right to become a state if the area's largely Mormon population did not stop practicing polygamy. After this case, the Mormon Church urged all its followers to obey the law and abandon polygamy, and Utah gained statehood.[16]

Disturbing the Peace or Preaching?

The passage of the Fourteenth Amendment made it easier for people to ask for the rights guaranteed by the Free Exercise Clause of the First Amendment. One significant case involving the right to free exercise of religion was known as *Cantwell* v. *Connecticut* in 1940.

Newton Cantwell and his sons belonged to the group known as Jehovah's Witnesses, which encourages its members to preach door-to-door. They were preaching in a largely Catholic neighborhood when they were arrested for disturbing the peace. The Supreme Court ruled that their arrest violated their First Amendment free speech and free exercise rights. Their message was considered to be protected religious speech.[17]

Religious Instruction in School

The issue of religious instruction in school did not come up for almost two centuries after the founding of the nation because the nation did not have a unified school system until the late nineteenth century. How much religion was incorporated into a school's daily lessons was usually determined on a local basis.

In 1940, Jewish, Roman Catholic, and some Protestant groups in Champaign, Illinois, formed a council on religious education. The group offered voluntary classes in religion to public school students. The classes took place during the day at school, and students who did not attend had to study something else.[18]

Vashti McCollum, a mother whose child attended a Champaign school, filed a lawsuit because her son James was teased when he did not attend the religion classes. She also said the classes were a waste of taxpayers' money, discriminated against minority faiths, and were unconstitutional.[19]

The Supreme Court ruled that using the state's tax-supported public school system to help religious groups provide religious education violated the First Amendment. Because of the Fourteenth Amendment, this also applied to states.[20]

Busing Children to Religious Schools

If students could not receive religious instruction in school, then perhaps they could be dismissed early to receive it somewhere else. That was the reasoning New York State used to avoid a lawsuit similar to *McCollum* v. *Board of Education*. So New York began a program in which public school students could be dismissed from class for religious teaching at another location. Those who did not attend had to stay in school.

However, a man named Tessim Zorach believed that excusing children for religious instruction violated the Establishment Clause of the First Amendment by promoting religion. When the case, *Zorach* v. *Clauson*, reached the Supreme Court, the justices ruled 6–3 that the New York program was different from the Illinois program. According to the Court, it did not establish religion and did not interfere with anyone freely expressing it. No public spaces were being used, and students were not being forced to do anything religious.[21]

In his opinion, Justice William Douglas, speaking for the majority, wrote:

We are a religious people whose institutions presuppose a Supreme Being. We guarantee the freedom to worship as one chooses. We make room for a wide variety of beliefs and creeds, as the spiritual needs of man deem necessary. We sponsor an attitude on the part of government that shows no partiality to any one group and that lets each flourish according to the zeal of adherents and the appeal of its dogma. When the state encourages religious instruction or cooperates with religious authorities, it follows the best of our traditions.[22]

In a related case, *Everson* v. *Board of Education*, Justice Hugo Black used Jefferson's phrase "a wall of separation between church and state" in his majority opinion. In that case, the Court voted 5–4 in favor of upholding a New Jersey plan to reimburse schools for busing students to private religious schools. A state court had ruled the plan unconstitutional.

Justice Black said that because the busing plan applied to both public and private schools, it did not breach the Establishment Clause of the First Amendment. Busing children to and from school is considered a public service given for their protection, no matter what religion they were or where they were going. Busing kept all children safe, just as police and fire departments protected all institutions—religious and secular.

Justice Wiley Blount Rutledge, writing for the minority, said that using tax money this way supported religious training and was unconstitutional.

Using the Fourteenth Amendment, the Court said that all states must define their laws by the Establishment Clause. Ultimately, the Court ruled that as long as money was not given directly to religious schools, funding transportation was okay.[23]

All of these cases helped to set the stage for one of the most controversial rulings on religion and public life, *Engel* v. *Vitale*, in 1962.

Much of the controversy about religion in public life has focused on public schools. Perhaps the most controversial of these cases involving schools is the *Engel* v. *Vitale* case of 1962, which would end teacher-led prayer in public schools.

When the Founding Fathers wrote the Constitution, there was no nationwide public school system and most schools were religious, so the question of a standardized national school system promoting religion never came up.

It was not until the mid-nineteenth century that Horace Mann, a teacher and education reformer in Massachusetts, began calling for a system of common schools.[1]

The "common-school" movement spread, and by 1918, every state required children to complete elementary school. Religion from a Protestant point of view played a daily part in classrooms. Teachers usually began the day by leading students in the Pledge of Allegiance, a prayer, a patriotic song, and a Bible reading.[2]

The Regents Prayer

In the early 1950s, the United States was engaged in a cold war with Communist nations, which had outlawed religion. There was also a strong movement to prevent the spread of communism in the United States. One way to do that seemed to be to promote religion. The New York State Board of Regents, which sets state education standards, recommended that public school students recite this prayer

Perhaps the most controversial of these cases involving schools is the *Engel* v. *Vitale* case of 1962, which would end teacher-led prayer in public schools.

every day: "Almighty God, we acknowledge our dependence upon Thee, and we beg Thy blessings upon us, our parents, our teachers, and our Country."

It was thought that this nondenominational prayer could not possibly offend anyone, and no child was required to say it if he or she did find it offensive. In July 1958, teachers in the Union Free School District Number 9, Town of North Hempstead, New York, began reading the prayer.[3]

It may not have offended many students, but some parents were concerned. When Steven Engel visited his son's Union Free School District classroom that year, he saw him bent over his desk with his hands clasped. He was reciting the Regent's Prayer, and Engel, who was Jewish, objected.

"I asked him, 'What were you doing?'" said Engel. "He said, 'I was saying my prayers.' I said, 'That's not the way we say prayers.'"

While children did not have to say the Regents Prayer, his son had been motivated to join in with his classmates. To Engel, this was a case of a school promoting religion and thereby influencing his son.

Meanwhile, at the same school, Lawrence Roth's sons, Daniel and Joseph, had chosen not to pray with their classmates and were allowed to leave the room during the prayer. As a result, their classmates insulted them and provoked fistfights.[4]

Leading the Class in Prayer

Steven Engel, Lawrence Roth, and other parents took the case to court. The case, which went all the way to the U.S. Supreme Court, known as *Engel* v. *Vitale*. (William Vitale was the school board president in the district.) In 1962, the Court voted 6–1 in favor of the parents. Requiring students to say prayers written by the state was now illegal.[5]

"In this country," Justice Hugo Black wrote in his opinion, "it is no part of the business of government to compose official prayers for any group of the American people to recite as part of a religious program carried on by government."[6] He also said, "It is a matter of history that this very practice of establishing governmentally composed prayers for religious services was one of the reasons which caused many of our early colonists to leave England and seek religious freedom in America."[7]

The Court's decision generated outrage. The plaintiffs received threatening messages, and a burning cross was left on the Roth family's lawn. The plaintiffs received postcards that said: "You damn Jews with your liberal viewpoint are ruining a wonderful country." (Actually, only two of the plaintiffs were Jewish; the others included a Unitarian, a member of the Ethical Culture Society, and an agnostic.[8])

This decision did not just generate anger against the parents who brought the case to court. Fury was directed at the presiding justice as well. Some people thought that states should be able to make their own decisions about what was taught in school. Others continue to blame the *Engel* v. *Vitale* ruling for the problems that some schools have today. Several movements to restore prayer through an additional amendment to the Constitution have been started, but they have never succeeded.

In Good Conscience

In 1956, when sixteen-year-old Ellery Schempp attended Abington High School in Abington, Pennsylvania, his school day always started with ten verses of the Bible and the Lord's

The Supreme Court ruled official classroom prayers unconstitutional in 1962. These Massachusetts students were photographed in 1980 participating in student-led prayer.

Prayer. At first, Schempp had no opinion about the readings, but as he learned more about the Constitution, he realized the readings probably violated the First Amendment. He thought that if he pointed it out to the school, they might just change the program.

"I had no idea it was going to be a court case, much less a Supreme Court case," said Schempp.

One morning when the prayer was read, he told the teacher that in good conscience, he could no longer stand for it. His family encouraged him to write to the ACLU, which took on his case. A federal court ruled that students could excuse themselves and sit in the hall when the readings took place, but a further case said that was too much like a punishment. The case went to the Supreme Court as *Abington Township* v. *Schempp and Murray* v. *Curlett.*

In 1963, the Court ruled 8–1 against the reading of Bible verses, finding that the readings and recitations could be considered religious ceremonies and were "intended by the State to be so."[9]

What About a Moment of Silence?

Many states tried to find ways around the ruling or ignored it altogether. An Alabama law said that every school day should begin with a voluntary prayer or moment of meditation.

In 1982, Ishmael Jaffree of Mobile, Alabama, filed a complaint on behalf of his three children. He said that two of the children had been subjected to various acts of religious indoctrination since kindergarten, that every day teachers led their classes in saying prayers, and that his children were insulted by or shunned by their classmates if they did not participate. And, he said, he had repeatedly but unsuccessfully requested that such acts be stopped.

"I brought the case because I wanted to encourage toleration among my children. I certainly did not want teachers who have control over my children for at least eight hours over the day to program them into any religious philosophy," said Jaffree.[10]

In stating the majority opinion, Justice John Paul Stevens said, "The First Amendment was adopted to curtail Congress' power to interfere with the individual's freedom to believe, to worship, and to express himself in accordance with the dictates of his own conscience, and the Fourteenth Amendment imposed the same substantive limitations on the States' power to legislate."[11]

Just saying that prayer was voluntary in a public school setting could be considered discriminatory because it implied that prayer was something you ought to do and something the schools gave their official seal of approval to. Even designating a moment of silence could make someone who did not want to pray feel uncomfortable or intimidated. The only way to be sure you were not intimidating students into praying was to not mention it at all.

"The addition of [the language] 'or voluntary prayer' indicates that the State intended to characterize prayer as a favored practice," the Court wrote. "Such an endorsement is not consistent with the established principle that the government must pursue a course of complete neutrality toward religion," said Stevens.[12]

Doesn't Graduation Deserve a Prayer?

While many students may say a prayer of thanks that they made it to their graduation ceremony, the courts have ruled that there can be no official prayer read at such ceremonies.

The case that brought this to court was *Lee* v. *Weisman* in 1992. In 1989, Deborah Weisman graduated from Nathan Bishop Middle School in Providence, Rhode Island. It had been customary for the school to invite members of the clergy to say a prayer at middle school and high school graduations. Even though Deborah's father, Daniel Weisman, objected to any prayers at the ceremony, the school invited Rabbi Leslie Gutterman to recite a nonsectarian prayer.

After the ceremony, Daniel Weisman filed a complaint, and the case reached the Supreme Court in 1992. In a 5–4 decision, the court ruled that the school's rule forced students to participate and act in ways that establish a state religion. The government may not compose an official religion. The court ruled against the school using what is known as the *Lemon* test.[13]

The *Lemon* test is based on a 1971 case known as *Lemon* v. *Kurtzman,* and it established the basis for judging all Establishment Clause cases afterward. The case concerned Pennsylvania and Rhode Island programs that supplemented the salaries of teachers in religious private schools because they were teaching secular (nonreligious) subjects. In order to pass the *Lemon* test and not violate the Establishment Clause, a law must have the following three characteristics:

- It must have a secular purpose.
- The law's primary effect must neither advance nor inhibit religion.
- The law must not excessively entangle the government with religion.[14]

According to the Supreme Court, prayers at graduation ceremonies did not pass the *Lemon* test.

Praying to Win

Can prayers be a part of a school's pregame warm-up? Not officially, found the ruling in the *Santa Fe Independent School District* v. *Doe* case in 2000.

Before the ruling, a student elected as Santa Fe High School's student council chaplain delivered a prayer over the public-address system before each football game. Two families filed a suit.

In a 6–3 opinion by Justice John Paul Stevens, the Supreme

Court held that permitting student-led, student-initiated prayer at football games violates the Establishment Clause. The prayers were ruled to be public speech authorized by a government's policy on government property atgovernment-sponsored events.

Such speech is not considered to be private, wrote Justice Stevens. In the opposing opinion, Chief Justice William H. Rehnquist said the Court's opinion seemed to display "hostility to all things religious in public life."[15]

Praying in School

After all these rulings, you may wonder if schools can tell students not to pray. They cannot. The only prayers that are forbidden are those sponsored by or promoted by the school.

Although the Constitution says public officials cannot direct or encourage prayer, students also have constitutional rights. They do not leave those rights behind when they go to school. Like everyone else, students have freedom of speech and freedom of religious expression. Nothing in the Constitution says that students cannot pray before, during, or after the school day.

According to the U.S. Department of Education guidelines, students are as free to pray with fellow students during the school day as they are to talk to them. That is, they may pray when they are not involved in school activities. Schools may not discriminate against prayer or religious speech. What students say at school is not government sponsored just because it is said in a public setting and to a public audience.[16]

According to Charles Haynes, author of *Finding Common Ground: A Guide to Religious Liberty in the Public Schools:*

> Religion has come into the public schools in all kinds of ways.… Many schools now understand that students have religious liberty rights in a public school, so you can go to many public schools today and kids will be giving each other religious literature, they

Football players pray before a game in Texas in 2006. In 2000, the Supreme Court ruled that official prayers violate the Establishment Clause.

will be sharing their faith. You go to most public schools now and see kids praying around the flagpole before school.[17]

Students will say, "Meet you at the flagpole" when they want to pray, and many groups meet there to say a prayer before school starts. There is also an annual event named See You at the Pole. The student-led movement started in Burleson, Texas, in 1990 with a small group of students. By 2006, more than two million teenagers met for See You at the Pole in all fifty states. Churches promote the event.[18]

In some schools, praying before the day starts can seem like an act of rebellion. For example, at West High School in Cedar

Falls, Iowa, a group of students has met at the flagpole every Wednesday for two years. The group met to pray and read the Bible. They also say brief prayers daily at their lockers before school starts.

"We are spending our Wednesday mornings for a reason," said sophomore Danny Lewis, a group member. "And in a way, ruining our reputations."

Taking a public stand for prayer can bring unwelcome attention from peers, just like taking a stand against it. Despite schools permitting the activities of such prayer groups, some conservative Christians still feel their right to pray is being curtailed. It can seem especially unfair to many because most of their neighbors share their religious beliefs.[19]

Nebraska students take part in the annual "See You at the Pole" event. Students have the constitutional right to freedom of religious expression as long as it does not interfere with the learning process.

Bobby Clanton, a school prayer activist from Mississippi, says the majority of students in his state are conservative Christians. If they want to pray, why shouldn't they? "We're tired of yielding to a tiny minority."[20]

Following the Law

Some schools assume that the Supreme Court rulings on school prayer do not apply to their situation. For example, a recent lawsuit says that a Delaware school district ignored First Amendment rulings by favoring one religion over the other.

At Samantha Dobrich's 2004 graduation from the Indian River School District, she was the only Jewish student in her graduating class. A local pastor said a prayer requesting heavenly guidance for the graduates, noting, "I also pray for one specific student, that you will be with her and guide her in the path that you have for her. And we ask all these things in Jesus' name."[21]

Samantha Dobrich felt that her graduation was ruined. Her parents and another set of parents filed a lawsuit saying that the school had ignored the *Lee* v. *Weisman* ruling on prayer at graduation. They claimed that school had also discriminated in other ways, such as:

- giving preferential treatment to students who joined Bible clubs
- distributing Bibles in school
- praying at sports and social events
- giving students a choice of attending a class in evolution or Bible club
- discussing Christianity in school, but no other religion

When Mona Dobrich, Samantha's mother, complained about the graduation prayer, school board members at first refused to put it on the agenda. The school eventually offered the compromise of saying a nondenominational prayer at graduation, which is also unconstitutional. Callers to a local radio station said the family should convert or leave the area and that the Ku Klux Klan, a secret terrorist society that promotes white supremacy and Protestantism, was nearby. The family felt so threatened that they moved.

"We are not trying to remove God from the schools or the public square," said Mona Dobrich. "We simply don't think it is right for the district to impose a particular religious view on impressionable students."[22]

The lawsuit has not yet come to trial.

I Pledge Allegiance

Americans pledge allegiance to the flag of the United States to show their loyalty to their country. The pledge they say reads: "I pledge allegiance to the flag of the United States of America, and to the Republic for which it stands, one Nation under God, indivisible, with liberty and justice for all."

Very few nations have such a pledge of loyalty, and it has not always been said in the United States. Before the early twentieth century, there was no pledge and no salute to the flag. The federal government did not endorse any guidelines for the pledge until 1942.

Since the pledge was written, many people have refused to recite it. Most reasons are either religious or political. People have refused to pledge because they say their religion does not allow them to pay respect to graven images. People have refused because they say the salute promotes a warlike attitude. Others refused as a way of protesting what they say is wrong with the U.S. government. For example, some people have protested because they did not think the United States really provides "liberty and justice for all."

The Pledge of Allegiance originally appeared in a children's magazine, *Youth's Companion*, in 1892. It was created by a staff writer and former Baptist minister named Francis Bellamy. Bellamy considered himself a Christian Socialist; his socialist

Other Incidents of Students Refusing to Pledge Allegiance

- In 1918, a nine-year-old Mennonite girl in West Liberty, Ohio, refused to pledge allegiance and was sent home. The Mennonites, a religious group, believe in nonviolence. This continued day after day until her father was sentenced to jail time for poisoning her mind.

- In 1925, thirty-eight Mennonite children were expelled from a Delaware school for refusing to say the pledge, since the pledge violated their religious beliefs. The Mennonite community started its own school to avoid the children being labeled truant.

- In 1926, fifty children belonging to a group called the Jehovites (different from the Jehovah's Witnesses) were expelled, but the children were allowed to return to school and not pledge.[23]

views had led to his resignation from the ministry. Bellamy wrote the pledge in response to a movement in the 1880s to have a flag wave over every schoolhouse in the nation. It originally read: "I pledge allegiance to my Flag and the Republic for which it stands, one nation indivisible, with liberty and justice for all."[24] In 1923, the words *my flag* were changed to "the flag of the United States of America."

Not everyone was enthusiastic about having to pledge allegiance in school. In 1935, William Gobitas, age ten, and Lillian Gobitas, twelve, were expelled from a school in Minersville, Pennsylvania, because they refused to salute the flag. The children were Jehovah's Witnesses, and their faith says they should not salute the flag, bear arms, or take part in politics or government. They could not salute the flag because they believed it to be a graven image or idol.

"I do not salute the flag because I have promised to do the will of God," wrote William in a letter to the board of the Minersville School District.[25]

Because the Gobitas family refused to salute, they were

considered unpatriotic. The children were physically attacked and the family's grocery store was boycotted.[26]

The *Minersville School District* v. *Gobitis* case reached the Supreme Court in 1940. (The case misspelled the family's last name.) The Court ruled against the family. The lone dissenting justice, Harlan Stone, argued that forcing students to say the pledge did violate the free exercise of religion guaranteed by the First Amendment, saying, "The state seeks to coerce these children to express a sentiment which . . . violates their deepest religious convictions."[27]

In the year that followed the *Gobitis* ruling, thousands of students who were Jehovah's Witnesses were expelled from school for refusing to pledge.[28] Rumors spread that the Jehovah's Witnesses were Nazi agents. This was unfounded; in actuality, Jehovah's Witnesses were being persecuted in Nazi Germany for refusing to pledge loyalty to Adolf Hitler. Because of the *Gobitis* ruling, many Jehovah's Witnesses in the United States were discriminated against and physically attacked.[29]

In 1942, the federal government officially recognized the Pledge of Allegiance. The West Virginia Board of Education adopted a resolution,

Schoolchildren salute the flag in 1942, before the words "under God" were added to the pledge of allegiance.

based on the Court's *Gobitis* opinion, that all schools teach courses in history and the Constitution and that saluting the flag become a regular part of the daily activity. All teachers and pupils were required to take part. Refusal would be considered an act of insubordination and could lead to being expelled from school.[30]

However, in 1943, the *Gobitis* ruling was reversed. In *West Virginia Board of Education* v. *Barnette*, the Supreme Court ruled that students could not be forced to pledge; the decision noted the similarity between the pledge and Hitler's salute. (Before World War II, the U.S. flag had been saluted with an outstretched arm. After the war, the pledge was recited with a hand placed over the heart.) Writing for the majority in the case, Justice Robert Jackson said that free public education should not be "partisan or enemy to any class, creed, party, or faction." The flag would continue to be saluted in schools but no student could be expelled for refusing to salute it.[31]

"Under God"

In 1954, the United States was engaged in a cold war with the Soviet Union, then a Communist nation that did not permit religious expression. Senator Joseph McCarthy launched a campaign to find all American Communist sympathizers. That year, at the request of President Dwight Eisenhower, Congress added the words *under God* to the pledge so it read: "I pledge allegiance to the Flag of the United States of America, and to the Republic for which it stands, one Nation under God, indivisible, with liberty and justice for all."[32] It was just a two-word addition, but it would be argued for decades to come.

Michael Newdow, the parent of a third grader in Sacramento, California, began a lawsuit in 2003 because he said that listening to those two words in the pledge violated his daughter's religious liberties. By law, she could not be forced to say the pledge, but if she did not, Newdow claimed, she would be singled out.

"Imagine you're a third-grader in a class of 30 kids. That's enormous pressure to put on a child," said Newdow. "Government needs to stay out of the religion business altogether."[33]

Newdow sued his daughter's school district in a case titled *Elk Grove Unified School District* v. *Newdow*. The Supreme Court considered his claim but eventually dismissed the case because Newdow was not the child's legal guardian and did not have the right to sue on her behalf. The ruling made many happy and left some feeling disappointed.

"The justices ducked this constitutional issue today, but it is likely to come back in the future," said the Reverend Barry W. Lynn, executive director of Americans United for Separation of Church and State. "Students should not feel compelled by school officials to subscribe to a particular religious belief in order to show love of country."[34]

A recent Associated Press poll found that nine in ten Americans want to keep the words *under God* in the pledge.[35]

Religion in School

Although schools cannot promote a religion, the Supreme Court has ruled that they can teach about religion and the contributions religion has made to history, literature, and law. The National School Boards Association has stated, "Study about religion is also important if students are to value religious liberty, the first freedom guaranteed in the Bill of Rights."[1] However, the group noted, religion must be taught in an objective and academic way:

- Students must not be forced to accept any religious teaching or be punished if they do not.

- Guest speakers such as ministers and rabbis may be invited to speak about their religion, but schools need to be sure that speakers understand that they can only share academic information.

- Teachers can talk to students about character issues such as the importance of telling the truth or helping other people, but they cannot involve religion in the discussion.

- Teachers themselves can pray in their free time, but they may not lead prayers in school or in after-school groups, since they would be seen as representing the school in leading those prayers.

- Teachers should not impose their religious beliefs in the classroom. If asked, they may answer the question briefly but not use the question to speak for or against religion.

- Students do have the freedom to share their views verbally and in written assignments.[2]

Reading the Bible

Even though teachers can inform children about the history of the Bible and its influence, schools may not have daily Bible readings. Bible reading in school was taken for granted until the mid-nineteenth century, when it sparked what are known as the Philadelphia Nativist Riots.

It was a time of great unrest in many American cities. The arrival of large numbers of Catholic immigrants from Ireland made it harder for many native-born people to find work. The immigrants were resented.

Economic unrest may have contributed to the riot that took place between native-born Protestant Philadelphians and Irish Catholic immigrants, which focused on reading the Bible in school. Irish Catholics felt that their children should not have to read from the Protestant King James version of the Bible, which was used by public schools. Catholic parents felt their children should be allowed to use their own version of the Bible or be excused altogether. When Catholic children began to leave the classroom during Bible reading, one teacher decided to suspend all religious instruction. Rumors spread that Catholics wanted to remove the Bible from school. This resulted in a violent clash that lasted several days, with twenty people killed and one hundred wounded.[3]

Public school children continued to read the King James edition of the Bible, and within a few years, a privately funded national system of Catholic schools was created, wherein children could receive a religious education.

The World's Most Hated Woman

Daily Bible readings were ruled unconstitutional, along with daily prayers, in *Abington* v. *Schempp* and *Murray* v. *Curlett*. The Murray in *Murray* v. *Curlett* was Madelyn Murray, a professed atheist, who felt that the Bible readings and Lord's Prayer her son, William, had to listen to in his Baltimore public school constituted a form of coercion. Coercion—forcing someone to do something they do not want to do—is a very important concept in many First Amendment cases.[4]

In general, adults find it easier to come to an objective decision than young children do. They have more experience to weigh information against. Young children tend to believe what they are told by adults. Through pressure from teachers or fellow students, a child may be forced into doing something he or she would not ordinarily do—like take part in a belief system that is different from that observed at home. That is why it is considered so important that children be protected from religious coercion.

In 1963, when William was fourteen, his mother demanded that school authorities excuse him from the classroom during Bible readings, prayers, and the Pledge of Allegiance. If they did not, she said, she would pull him out of school. The school refused, and William stayed home. The ACLU took the case but insisted William return to school. When he did, he was beaten up and called names by other children.[5]

After the *Abington* v. *Schempp* and *Murray* v. *Curlett* ruling, many people were furious with the Schempp and Murray families. Madelyn Murray came to symbolize all of the frustration felt by people who wanted the schools to continue teaching religion. She called herself "the most hated woman in America."[6]

William Murray is now a practicing Christian and author of the book *Let Us Pray: A Plea for Prayer in Our Schools*. He regrets his earlier involvement in the case and thinks that communities should be allowed to make their own policy about religion:

"I was the only student at Woodbourne Junior High who objected to prayer and Bible reading, yet the entire school was made to conform to my wishes. The principle can be taken too far: the minority can hold the majority hostage."[7] He also notes: "Local control guaranteed that the content of religious education in any particular school represented the prevailing sentiments in the community in which it was located."[8]

In his book, Murray states that the *Murray* v. *Curlett* ruling denies the country a valuable part of its heritage. He does not believe the Founding Fathers ever meant the First Amendment to be interpreted the way it was.

"While the authors of the First Amendment were still alive, and for generations after, religion played a vital role in America's public schools and in government itself," said Murray.[9]

Although the *Abington* v. *Schempp* and *Murray* v. *Curlett* case ruled against daily Bible reading in school, the Court's decision made a point of saying that learning about the Bible was not only permitted but something desirable.

"It might well be said that one's education is not complete without a study of comparative religion or the history of religion and its relationship to the advancement of civilization," said Associate Justice Tom Clark.[10]

Bringing the Bible to School

Contrary to what these cases might lead a person to believe, the courts did not bar Bible reading in school under all circumstances. Students can read their own Bibles in school, and the Bible can be studied and discussed both as literature and in the objective study of religion.

Schools may teach about the Bible as long as it is done from an educational point of view and not a religious one. For example, picking one version of the Bible over another would be taking a religious perspective. When discussing the Bible, teachers need to note that there are the Jewish Bible, or Hebrew Scriptures, and several Christian Bibles for Protestants, Catholics, and Orthodox Christians. Actions described in the Bible may not be described as historical fact.[11]

Straying from that definition is unconstitutional, and yet some school districts still ignore such guidelines. A recent study by the Texas Freedom Network, a civil-liberties group, says most elective Bible courses currently offered in twenty-five Texas school districts promote one faith above another.

"These efforts to push illegal Bible courses not only undermine religious freedom—they are also bad for religion. The last thing any Bible-believing person should want is state-sponsored Sunday school classes," said Charles Haynes, a First Amendment scholar.[12]

One problem with a state-sponsored Sunday-school class would be that the state would decide what the content of such a class would be. Persons of faith generally want to make that decision for themselves. With a growing diversity of

Students may read the Bible on their own in school and study it as literature.

religions in the United States, such a class would displease many people, including quite a few Christians. While Christians may be the largest religious group in the nation, there are many kinds of Christians. Each denomination may favor a different version of the Bible and have slightly different teachings. Which group would decide the curriculum? Which Bible would they choose? Who would have to attend and how would they have to participate?

"If history is any guide, we know that the surest way to destroy authentic faith is to turn it over to the government," says Haynes.[13]

Talking Up Your Faith

Proud to be a Christian? Or a Hindu? Or a Buddhist? Or a Wiccan? Speak right up, as long as you don't interrupt class-room time or invade the privacy of your fellow students. Even though the courts in First Amendment cases have ruled that schools cannot promote any religion, the same amendment guarantees that you have a right to express yours.

So does *Religious Expressions in Public Schools: A Statement of Principles* by the U.S. Department of Education. These guide-lines, which were created in 1995 under the direction of President Bill Clinton, say:

> The Establishment Clause of the First Amendment does not prohibit purely private religious speech by students. Students there-fore have the same right to engage in individual or group prayer and religious discussion during the school day as they do to engage in other comparable activity. For example, students may read their Bibles or other scriptures, say grace before meals, and pray before tests to the same extent they may engage in comparable non-dis-ruptive activities. Local school authorities possess substantial discretion to impose rules of order and other pedagogical restrictions on student activities, but they may not structure or administer such rules to discriminate against religious activity or speech.[14]

This means that students can pray or read the Bible when they have free time as long as they do not disturb other students or school activities. For example, a student can express his faith during a classroom discussion or in a written assignment, but he or she cannot get up in front of the class and deliver a lecture. Neither can he or she engage someone in a religious conversation if the other person is not willing to participate in such a discussion.[15]

In 2003, the administration of President George W. Bush issued new guidelines on religion in public schools. The guidelines state that schools cannot initiate prayer or religious speech but that students expressing themselves through prayer or in another form of religious expression may not be restricted because of the religious content of their speech. Schools that do not follow these guidelines may be denied funding from the federal government. Because these guidelines seem to contradict previous court rulings, which say students cannot be a captive audience for religious statements, they create confusion for teachers and administrators who want to follow the guidelines and let students express themselves but still worry about potential lawsuits.[16]

> The courts did not bar Bible reading in school under all circumstances. Students can read their own Bibles in school, and the Bible can be studied and discussed both as literature and in the objective study of religion.

For many experts, the Bush guidelines seem like a positive statement. According to First Amendment scholar Charles Haynes, who helped put the guidelines together, "We have more consensus today than we've ever had on how to deal with religion in the public schools. The bad news is that carrying out that consensus is difficult given the long history of controversy."[17]

American Muslims, Buddhists, Hindus, and Jews—people of all faiths, and people who have no religious beliefs—are free to practice and express their convictions, according to the U.S. Constitution.

Spreading the Word

If you want to distribute religious fliers at school, you can, as long as you clear it with school officials. Students can distribute religious literature if they respect the conditions set by their school. Although some students have complained school restrictions limit the time they can hand out literature and that this restricts students' free-speech rights, courts have said schools may make such decisions.

In a case known as *Hedges* v. *Wauconda Community Unit School District*, the court ruled that a junior high school could limit when and how students could pass out literature, as long as the limits were reasonable. Handing out religious literature cannot disrupt school, invade the privacy of other students, or be sponsored or endorsed by the school. In addition, the literature handed out cannot contain any obscenity or advertise products that are illegal for minors.[18]

While schools can decide which religious literature may be sent home with students, they cannot discriminate on the basis of religion. If fliers about a secular camp are being distributed, fliers about a religious camp may also be distributed. In 2000, the Scottsdale Unified School District in Phoenix denied Joseph Hills permission to distribute fliers on a religious summer camp.

In 2003, the Ninth Circuit Court, in *Hills* v. *Scottsdale Unified School District*, ruled that schools can't refuse to distribute literature for a religious program, but it can refuse to distribute literature that itself endorses religion.[19] The Supreme Court refused to hear the case, and this was considered a victory for those who thought religious groups had been denied their First Amendment right of free speech.

"Christians are no longer forced to ride on the back of the free speech bus," said Gary McCaleb, an ADF attorney.[20]

The Equal Access Act

The Equal Access Act of 1984 was designed to end what some saw as discrimination against religious clubs in public schools. The act has four parts:

- A school cannot discriminate between extracurricular student groups on the basis of religion. So, if a school says okay to the chess club, it also has to say okay to a Bible-reading club.

- The groups have to be started and led by students.
- The school can control group activities if necessary to maintain discipline or to protect students and faculty. The school can also decide when and where students can meet. Religious groups must meet in noninstructional time.

- Teachers can be present at meetings but not participate.

Young people are free to discuss their faith, distribute literature, and hold religious club meetings on school grounds as long as they follow school guidelines.

Participation would make it seem as if they were officially endorsing the club and its views.[21]

The act says:

It shall be unlawful for any public secondary school which receives Federal financial assistance and which has a limited open forum to deny equal access or a fair opportunity to, or discriminate against, any students who wish to conduct a meeting within that limited open forum on the basis of the religious, political, philosophical, or other content of the speech at such meetings.[22]

According to the act, student religious groups at public secondary schools have the same right to meet and use school facilities as other groups. Their meeting can include a prayer service, Bible reading, and other forms of worship. Schools can use the public-address system, the school newspaper, and bulletin boards to announce meetings. Students can meet during their lunch periods, as well as before and after the school day. These times are considered "open forum," since nothing is being taught then.[23]

Why Equal Access Is Important

In 1990, the Westside School District in Nebraska denied permission to a group of students who wanted to form a Christian club in their school. Faculty sponsors were required for all after-school activities, and the school decided that would seem like a school endorsement of a religious group. The students said the school was violating the Equal Access Act.

By an 8–1 ruling, the Supreme Court decided the students could have their club as long as it was student-initiated and student-led. Also, the sponsoring teacher could not be paid to help with the club, because that would mean the school endorsed the religious activity.[24]

Religious Clubs

Despite the existence of legislation such as the Equal Access Act, decades of court cases about religious expression in school have left school officials confused and cautious about the possibility of being sued. One such school was the Milford Central School in Milford, New York.

In September 1996, Stephen and Darleen Fournier, parents of a child in the school district, asked the school if they could use the cafeteria for weekly after-school meetings of the Good News Club, a Christian group for children aged six to twelve. In 1997, the school board rejected the application.

The case went to the Supreme Court as *Good News Club* v. *Milford Central School.* In 2000, the Supreme Court ruled 6–3 that the club had a free-speech right to hold its meetings there. Clubs could not be discriminated against because they were religious.[25]

Justice Clarence Thomas, writing for the majority, said, "We conclude that Milford's restriction violates the club's free speech rights and that no Establishment Clause concern justifies that violation."[26]

In a minority opinion, Justice David Souter said that the club's activities blurred the line between instruction and religious indoctrination, "leaving a reasonable elementary school pupil unable to appreciate that the former instruction is the business of the school while the latter evangelism is not."[27]

Religion in the Workplace

Students who work after school and during school breaks also have the right to express their faith in the workplace. According to the U.S. Equal Employment Opportunity Commission, Title VII of the Civil Rights Act of 1964 says employers may not treat employees more favorably or less favorably because of their religion. For example, an employer cannot refuse to hire someone because of that job candidate's religion.

Employees cannot be forced to participate in a religious activity; conversely, employers must permit employees to engage in religious expression, unless that expression creates a hardship for the employer. Employers must also prevent religious harassment in the workplace. That means no one can make fun of other people's religion or make life difficult for them because of their religious practices.[28]

Leaving School for Your Beliefs

Throughout the history of public education in the United States, a number of families have chosen to remove their children from public education because they felt it conflicted with their religious beliefs. Some families took their children from school because they felt it did not promote or support their religious values. A few families even homeschool their children because they feel public schools expose their children to more religious practices than they consider appropriate.

A pivotal case that involved the conflict between religious beliefs and compulsory state education was *Wisconsin* v. *Yoder*. The case came to trial in 1972 because members of two Amish communities withdrew their children from school, saying that their religion did not approve of public education after the eighth grade. The Amish are a Protestant religious group, founded in the 1690s, that shuns many modern inventions and values.

At that time, Wisconsin state law required that children attend school until the age of sixteen. Children who attend eighth grade are usually younger. The Amish communities object to school attendance past that age because they think that young people should spend these years preparing themselves for adult baptism, a religious and social ritual that makes them full members of the community.

The supreme court of Wisconsin decided that the free exercise of religion under the First Amendment was more important than the state's interest in making children attend school after the eighth grade. Chief Justice Warren E. Burger of the U.S. Supreme Court said that the values and programs of secondary school were "in sharp conflict with the fundamental mode of life mandated by the Amish religion," and that two more years of school would not add any benefits that would justify such a conflict.[29]

While the Court did not rule on the right of all parents to school their children at home, this case was followed by an increase in the number of parents who chose to do so. Homeschooling is legal in all states, although children must

This Virginia boy, shown in a library with his mother, is being homeschooled. Many parents homeschool their children to make sure they can impart their values.

meet certain standardized educational requirements to receive a high school diploma. It is estimated that more than a million children are homeschooled, a figure which is estimated to grow by at least 10 percent a year. While there are many reasons for homeschooling students—such as a child's special educational needs or safety issues—a common reason is that parents do not feel schools teach the values they believe in.[30]

For example, a parent might not be comfortable sending his or her child to a school that teaches evolution, the theory that genetic changes led earlier life-forms to evolve into human beings, but does not teach creationism, the view of the earth's creation found in the first chapter of the Bible. Some parents want religion to shape their children's education.

The Smalkowski family of Hardesty, Oklahoma, had no problem with the curriculum at their daughter's school, but they eventually chose to homeschool all three of their kids because religious practices at the school made the children uncomfortable. All the members of the Smalkowski family consider themselves atheists.

Nicole Smalkowski, the family's oldest daughter, joined the girls' basketball team in her high school and was upset to discover that after a game, team members gathered to recite the Lord's Prayer.

"I didn't think they had religion in sports," said Nicole. "But when it came to basketball they would pray before and after practices. They would pray during games."

Nicole did not feel comfortable bowing her head, so she stepped away from the prayer circle. After refusing to pray, she was accused of stealing a teammate's sneakers, which Nicole denies happened. She was kicked off the team for a whole year. When she was permitted to return, she still refused to pray, and a day later was suspended from school for allegedly threatening another student, which she also denies took place.[31]

The family sued the town, hoping to bar prayer before and

after games, and demanded that the school advise students that they have a constitutional right not to pray or participate in religious activities in school. The school insisted that it was one coach who required the prayers and the school no longer employed him. The district court ruled that since the coach was gone, there was no evidence that Nicole would be harmed.[32] The family decided to homeschool all three of their children.

"I miss school," said Nicole, who will now find it harder to qualify for an athletic scholarship. "But I don't wanna go back to that school. I tried going back to that school for two days, and I couldn't handle it. And there was a new kid there and he's like, 'Oh, I heard about you. You're that dirty little trouble-making atheist.'"[33]

Holiday Celebrations

Who's afraid of Halloween? School officials and parents alike have become fearful of the witches' brew of controversy that some traditional holiday celebrations stir up.

Halloween's roots date back to the Celtic harvest ritual of Samhain. In the first few centuries of the Christian Church, a day was designated to honor Christians who had died. As Christianity spread throughout Ireland, the Irish Christian Church came to observe this as All Saints Day on November 1. The night before, which had been celebrated as Samhain, became All Hallows Eve and eventually was known in the United States as Halloween.

Today, it's a holiday focused on dressing up in costumes and trick-or-treating door-to-door for candy. Traditional celebrations at schools have included costume parades and reading scary stories. Afraid of the potential controversy associated with this holiday's celebrations, many schools now play down Halloween and instead celebrate the fall season with activities that center around falling leaves and pumpkins.[1]

The complaints about Halloween celebrations have come from many corners. While Christian and Muslim parents have complained that the holiday is too pagan and too gory, Jewish parents have said the holiday is too Christian.

"Halloween is not a Jewish holiday," said Steven Soloman, a youth director at a New Jersey Jewish school. "It's All Saints' Day."[2]

In response to such complaints, some schools have trimmed down their celebrations, canceling parades but keeping the pumpkins. Other schools have chosen to make the celebration an after-school event so it would be easier for any families who did not want to participate.

In the Denver Palmer Elementary School, dress-up day was canceled because officials said it was too time-consuming. However, the school did sponsor a Halloween festival at night. "We get a very full night but those who want to opt out can," said principal Mike Crawford.[3]

Halloween is not the only holiday that generates complaints—and occasionally lawsuits. Most holiday complaints generally involve days celebrated in the month of December, when Christmas, Kwanzaa, and often Hanukkah take place.

Christmas is a Christian holiday that celebrates the birth of Jesus. Since no one knew exactly when Jesus was born, around the third century AD, the church decided to adopt the time originally set aside for the yearly Roman festival of Saturnalia. During the pagan Saturnalia festival, slaves were temporarily freed and people feasted. Christmas Day is an official federal holiday and schools are usually closed for the week.

Kwanzaa is a nonreligious African-American holiday that takes place from December 26 to January 1. Based on traditional African agricultural celebrations, it was created in 1966 by activist Ron Karenga.

Hanukkah, or the Festival of Lights, celebrates a miracle from the second century B.C.E. in which temple oil lasted eight days. Since the Jewish calendar is based on the lunar cycle, the dates do not coincide with the modern calendar; thus, Hanukkah can take place on different days during November or December.

Some people frown on any publicly funded religious celebrations. Some think there should be less emphasis on the religious aspects of the holidays, while others think it's okay as long as all cultures and religions are represented. Some accept virtually all forms of religious celebrations. According to the Alliance Defense Fund, 95 percent of Americans celebrate Christmas. Yet due to concern about offending minorities and the ever-present threat of lawsuits, schools are confused about what kinds of holiday celebrations are appropriate.[4]

To help understand this controversy, it may help to learn more about the nation's December holidays.

The December Dilemma

The Puritans disapproved of Halloween celebrations because they thought them pagan, but they especially disapproved of Christmas. In fact, they thought Christmas celebrations were so pagan that they fined anyone who observed the holiday. The records of the General Court of the Massachusetts Bay Colony said that whoever celebrated Christmas by feasting or not working "shall pay for every offence five shilling as a fine to the county." It took twenty-two years for an English-appointed governor to cancel the ban on Christmas.[5]

Mixed feelings about the holiday did not end when this ban was canceled. As late as 1855, some churches were closed on December 25 because they did not consider it a holy day. On the eve of the Civil War, only eighteen states recognized Christmas as an official holiday.[6]

Many of the symbols that have come to be associated with Christmas have not always been a part of the way Americans celebrate. For example, the original colonists did not have Christmas trees. The tradition of putting up a fir tree probably came to the United States with German immigrants who settled in Pennsylvania. The first written record of Christmas trees in the United States was dated 1821 in the diary of a Lancaster, Pennsylvania, resident.[7] The United States did not decorate a national Christmas tree until 1923, when President Calvin Coolidge lit a forty-eight-foot balsam in Washington, D.C.[8]

By the 1920s, department stores were promoting the idea that it could not really be Christmas without lots of presents. A 1931 roundup of sermons reported by *The New York Times* shared the point of view that Christmas had become too much about shopping and not enough about religion.[9]

Today, holiday symbols such as Christmas trees, lights, the colors red and green, television holiday commercials, Christmas music on the radio, and holiday supermarket displays in place before Halloween make it unlikely that anyone would forget Christmas was near.

Many people—Christians and non-Christians—enjoy all the music, decorations, and traditions associated with Christmas celebrations. Others, including some Christians, feel the holiday has become way too commercial. For some non-Christians, the season can make them feel like outsiders.

"You cannot go anywhere in December without being loudly reminded that Christmas is a large part of our culture and economy; but to a Jew it is different because it helps to emphasize how much we are not included in this aspect of America," said Jonathan Chisdes, editor of a Jewish publication, *L'Chaim.*[10]

Saint Nicholas to Santa Claus

For some people, Santa Claus has become a symbol of everything that is too commercial about Christmas. Yet Santa Claus started out as a Christian Turkish bishop named Saint Nicholas, honored for his good deeds, generosity, and faith. His day, December 6, is celebrated in many countries, including Italy, Greece, France, Germany, Austria, Switzerland, Belgium, and the Netherlands.[11] Dutch and German settlers brought the feast day of Saint Nicholas, or Sinterklaas, to the New World, where the trim saint became heftier and was renamed Santa Claus.

> Many of the symbols that have come to be associated with Christmas have not always been a part of the way Americans celebrate. For example, the original colonists did not have Christmas trees.

Some Christians see Santa as a nonreligious symbol. When it comes to holiday decorations, they do not think he is a valid substitute for a nativity scene, which portrays Jesus' birth. Conversely, many people of other faiths think that images of Santa Claus make holiday decorations Christian.

Is There a War Against Christmas?

In an effort to be inclusive and not offend anyone, it has become popular to refer to December celebrations as "the holidays." People say "happy holidays" or "season's greetings" and refer to decorations as "holiday decorations," even if these decorations focus on one specific holiday. A Christmas tree may be referred to as a "holiday tree" or a "giving tree."

When Larry Black, principal of Bowsher High School in

South Toledo, Ohio, referred to his school's decorations as a Christmas tree, he quickly corrected himself and referred to it as a "holiday tree."

"We try to respect everybody's beliefs," said Black. "The music department does a Christmas concert. Well, actually it's a holiday concert."[12]

Such efforts to include everyone have made some Christians furious. Why should they have to give up a cherished tradition? John Gibson, author of *The War on Christmas*, says:

> Christians have a right to put up a Christmas tree in school and call it what it is. They shouldn't have to call it a "paradise tree" or a "friendship tree" or a "giving tree" or a "world tree" or a "holiday tree" just because it's in a public place any more than Jews should have to call a menorah (which represents a religious miracle to them) a "holiday candelabra" in case Christians or atheists are offended.[13]

A Christmas Break?

Are schools allowed to even mention Christmas? In 2000, the Covington, Georgia, school board was notified that the ACLU would take it to court if the school board members used the word Christmas on their school calendar. Afraid of a lawsuit, the board changed the name to winter break.

"To call it a Christmas break would be endorsing one religion over the other, which would be Christianity over other religions or the absence of religion," said Craig Goodmark, an ACLU lawyer.

However, according to the National School Boards Association, if schools close because a percentage of children who observe certain religions won't be there, it's not an endorsement of a religion. A majority of students in the United States are Christian, so school is closed during the Christmas holiday.[14]

Such calendar accommodations also happen on other days

in areas where other holidays are likely to lower school attendance. For example, in the New York metropolitan area, public schools are closed for the Jewish holy days Yom Kippur and Rosh Hashanah, because school officials know that many students and teachers will stay home to observe the holiday.

So far, no school districts have made allowances for Muslim holidays, but that may also change as the Muslim population in the United States grows. There are now 5 to 7 million Muslims in the United States. One of the nation's fastest growing populations, it is expected that by 2010, the number of Muslims in the United States will be greater than the Jewish population.[15]

Muslim leaders in one Baltimore, Maryland, school district have asked that all Maryland students be given two floating holidays, so that Muslim students could observe the holy days of Eid al-Fitr and Eid al-Adha without worrying about being marked absent or missing important tests. Some of the area schools close for Yom Kippur and Rosh Hashanah. Although Muslim students may stay home for a holy day and it is considered an excused absence, parents say that even an excused absence is an absence.[16]

Schools have the liberty to arrange their own holiday schedules but must have a minimum number of teaching days every year. Many districts are looking for ways to make their schedules more flexible.

Banishing Christmas?

Attempts to make the December holidays more inclusive have been seen by some as an attempt to do away with Christmas. Feeling that Christmas was threatened, groups such as the American Family Association have taken action. For example, in 2005, the association asked people not to shop in Target stores, because the chain did not use the phrase "Merry Christmas" in their decorations and advertisements.[17]

"The right to freely exercise one's faith has never been more threatened in our nation than it is today," says the Alliance Defense Fund Web site. "And the rights of Christians are especially vulnerable."[18]

This organization launched a boycott to change the minds of merchants. In Raleigh, North Carolina, a church paid $7,600 for an advertisement urging Christians to shop at merchants' stores that used the words "Merry Christmas" in their advertisements. A California-based group boycotted Macy's department stores because the store used the saying "Season's Greetings," even though clerks could say "Merry Christmas" to customers if they chose to. For some Christians, saying "Happy Holidays" misses the message.

A holiday scene in front of city hall in Jersey City, New Jersey. Courts have found such scenes legal if they do not serve to endorse one religion over another.

Should stores have to say "Merry Christmas" when their owners are not Christian or they prefer to acknowledge more than one holiday celebration? Should stores be boycotted and lose business if they don't say "Merry Christmas"? Isn't punishing them for not wanting to say "Merry Christmas" and celebrate a Christian holiday a form of discrimination? In Raleigh, North Carolina, one minister, the Reverend Jim Melynk of St. Mark's Episcopal Church, compared such boycotts to the way Nazis used to make Jewish merchants put yellow stars on their store fronts. That way the Nazis would immediately know who was and who wasn't Christian.[19]

A holiday that promotes "peace on earth and good will to men" has generated considerable hostility.

Public Holiday Displays

When setting up a holiday display on public land, is it okay to display Santa and his reindeer? Can the community have a nativity scene and a menorah? How about a menorah alone? What seasonal symbols can be displayed on school and other government property? Here are some rulings that the courts have made:

- The city of Pawtucket, Rhode Island, traditionally put up a Christmas display in its shopping district. The display included a Santa Claus house, a Christmas tree, a banner reading "Season's Greetings," and a nativity scene. A Pawtucket resident, Daniel Donnelly, sued the mayor, Dennis Lynch, saying the city violated the First Amendment. In 1984, in a 5–4 decision, the Supreme Court said the city had not violated the Establishment Clause of the First Amendment because it did not advocate a specific religious message.[20]

- The American Civil Liberties Union challenged two public holiday displays in Pittsburgh, Pennsylvania. One case focused on a nativity scene inside the Allegheny County Courthouse. The second display was a large Hanukkah menorah that Chabad, a Jewish organization, placed outside the city-county building. The ACLU said both holiday displays were examples of the state endorsing religion.

The Supreme Court said, in a 5–4 decision, that the nativity scene endorsed Christianity and violated the Establishment Clause because it used the words "Glory to God in the highest" in Latin. However, not all religious displays on government property are illegal, according to the Court. The menorah was permitted.[21]

The Court declared the nativity scene in the courthouse to be unconstitutional because it was a stand-alone Christmas display, not because it had any particular words on it. The Court declared the menorah to be constitutional because it accompanied a Christmas tree and a sign by the mayor, which praised liberty. The issue in this case was whether there is a constitutional difference in religious symbols on public property when one symbol is a stand-alone religious symbol and the other is in a display that contains symbols of more than one religion. Even though the Court's ruling wanted to be fair, it caused some people to feel one religion was being favored over another.

Evolving School Policies

When trying to change the way holidays are observed in schools, some district policies have met strong opposition from the communities they are based in. Voters in the Mustang, Oklahoma, school district were so angry at their school board for removing a traditional nativity scene from their school Christmas play that in the next election residents voted against funding the school had requested. Some parents were upset that

Santa Claus, a Christmas tree, and Hanukkah symbols were approved, but not a nativity scene. When the play was performed, one hundred people protested outside, carrying signs that said: "No Christ. No Christmas. Know Christ. Know Christmas."

"If you're going to cut one symbol, then cut them all," said Shelly Marino, the parent of a third grader in the school.[22]

The school system did not reinstate the nativity scene, but five months after the play did create a religious liberty policy that would cover all future related events. The policy's preamble states:

> Public schools may neither instill nor inhibit religion. They must be places where religion and religious conviction are treated with fairness and respect. Mustang Public Schools uphold the First Amendment by protecting the religious liberty rights of students of all faiths or no faith. The proper role of religion in the public school curriculum is academic and not devotional.[23]

The school promised to investigate and resolve any complaints regarding religious freedom of expression but did not specifically mention holiday concerts.

"If we had had this policy in place, we would not have had any issue come up in December. It provides us with an opportunity to be able to teach about religion, and that makes all the difference," said school superintendent Karl Springer.[24]

Sharing the Spirit

Can a student personally express his religion by giving out religious holiday cards? Justin Cortez, a kindergarten student at North Gresham Grade School in Gresham, Oregon, attended a class Christmas party where students could bring cards and gifts to exchange. He chose a card with a candy cane on it that contained a story about the meaning of the candy cane: It said that it was in the shape of a J, which stood for Jesus, and that the white stood for "the pureness of Jesus," the red for "the blood

Jesus shed for us." When a teacher saw the card, she showed it to school officials, who said Justin could not distribute the card in school because it might be interpreted as endorsing religion.

The American Center for Law and Justice filed a lawsuit on behalf of Justin and his mother. The lawsuit said that forbidding Justin from expressing his religious beliefs violated the principles of the First Amendment and that the school had failed to protect his religious beliefs.[25]

The case ended with a settlement. In the future, the school district will not let students hand out cards with a religious message to students, but teachers can let students know they are on a table in the room and students can pick them up if they like.[26]

Christmas Greetings and Hymns

While students may be allowed to take part in any holiday celebrations they like, they cannot be forced to celebrate a holiday. Concerns over this are nothing new. In 1905, during the Christmas season, the principal of a predominantly Jewish school in Brooklyn, New York, urged all the children in his school to be "like Christ."

When thirteen-year-old Augusta Herman pointed out that such teaching was more appropriate for a Sunday school, the principal insulted her. Inspired by the fact that a student had taken a stand, the Union of Orthodox Hebrew Congregations asked the New York City Board of Education to make sure the schools were not teaching Christianity. The board responded that Christmas observations would continue.

As a result, a local Jewish newspaper called for a boycott on December 24. Between 20,000 and 25,000 students stayed home. Two weeks later, the city's elementary school committee recommended that schools ban the singing of Christmas hymns and the assignment of Christmas essays.[27]

Few schools were predominantly Jewish in 1905, and few schools are today. Yet within a century, an increasingly diverse population caused many of the nation's schools to consider and reconsider their December musical choices. In 2004, Columbia High School in Maplewood, New Jersey, decided to ban the singing of Christmas carols in its December school concert. The brass band had to confine itself to seasonal musical numbers such as "Frosty the Snowman" and "Walking in a Winter Wonderland."[28]

Jessica Schneider, a sixteen-year-old member of the school's ensemble band, thought the ban was "kind of silly." She said: "Personally, I don't know anyone who objected, and as a student who's part of the school's Jewish population, I would think I would have. To me it's just music and it's giving the community something to be happy about."[29]

Apparently so did other residents. A crowd of one hundred carolers, including several Orthodox Jews, stood before the school and sang Christmas and Hanukkah songs.

"The greatest works of art in Western civilization are inspired by religious predominantly Christian— convictions," said caroler Susan Rosenbluth, editor of *Jewish Voice and Opinion*, a monthly publication based in Englewood, New Jersey.[30]

Richard Thompson, chief

A rabbi and boy read prayers for Rosh Hashanah, the Jewish New Year, in New York of 1907. Two years earlier, Jewish students had boycotted the New York City schools to protest the teaching of Christianity.

counsel of the Thomas More Law Center, said that the Maplewood policy was "another example of the anti-Christmas, anti-religious policy." The center is a not-for-profit public interest law firm dedicated to the defense and promotion of the religious freedom of Christians. Thompson said the school had originally acted on complaints from parents, but by getting rid of a whole category of music just because it is religious, the school's ban may actually be unconstitutional. It may violate the Establishment Clause.[31]

The Maplewood school district banned holiday music to conform to their understanding of the law and avoid a potential lawsuit but then was sued by the Thomas More Law Center, on behalf of two Maplewood students, Kurt and Karl Stratechuk, who felt their ability to freely express their faith was being denied. The lawsuit was dismissed.

To reduce the possibility of any further disputes, the school district redefined its policy in 2005 to say: "Music programs prepared or presented by student groups as an outcome of the curriculum shall not have a religious orientation or focus on religious holidays."[32]

A Spirit of Respect

Do schools have to avoid talking about religion in December or incorporating religion into any programs? What about Christmas music?

"Of course not," says First Amendment Scholar Charles Haynes. "A concert in December without any sacred music makes little sense. Much of Western music had its origins in religious practice and belief. Surely traditional Christmas carols and other Christmas music by composers such as Bach and Handel should have a place in any good public school music curriculum."[33]

Here are just a few guidelines from the First Amendment

Center, which works to preserve and protect constitutionally guaranteed freedoms through information and education:

- Holiday concerts may include music related to Christmas, Hanukkah, and other religious traditions, but religious music may not dominate.

- Dramatic productions should emphasize the cultural aspects of the holidays. Plays about the nativity or the Hanukkah miracle would not be appropriate.

- While recognizing the holiday season, none of the school activities in December should have the purpose or effect of promoting or inhibiting religion.[34]

When planning a holiday program, school administrators and teachers should ask:

- Is there a clear educational purpose? Under the First Amendment, learning about religious holidays is an appropriate goal; celebrating them is not.

- Will any student be made to feel like an outsider?

- Is the overall curriculum fair?[35]

There are many opportunities for education in seasonal celebrations that respect religious heritage without promoting any particular religion. Finding them may be a challenge for teachers, but the results can be very worthwhile.

Sandra Conch, a teacher in Lititz, Pennsylvania, uses food, decorations, stories, and music to celebrate the diversity of holiday traditions. Her students share their own holiday traditions with their classmates and thereby learn to appreciate the practices of others.

"Our traditions and rituals shape who we are as a people and a society. So the more we know, understand and respect each other's rituals, the greater our chances of living in harmony," said Couch."[36]

Symbols of Faith

In 2004, the French government passed a law saying that public school students would be expelled if they showed up at school wearing the head scarves favored by Muslim women, the yarmulkes, or skullcaps, worn by orthodox Jewish men, the turbans worn by Sikh men, or any large Christian crosses. The law forbidding all religiously conspicuous clothing was designed to maintain France's laws separating church and state.[1]

The law concerning the wearing of religious symbols may have been drafted as a response to a growing concern among many people that immigrant Muslims were not adopting French cultural customs. Approximately five million Muslims live in France, and an increasing number of French Muslim girls were arriving at school wearing headscarves, known as hijab.[2]

Before the law was passed, French parents had to notify the school if their daughter was going to wear a headscarf. In 1989, there were only ten children signed up to wear headscarves. By 1994, there were two thousand. French officials feared that a growing number of children wearing different clothes might divide rather than unite the country.[3]

Many Muslims believe that a girl should dress modestly and cover herself when she reaches adolescence. This can range from wearing a hijab to being completely covered from head to toe, except for the eyes.[4]

While some non-Islamic countries restrict the wearing of headscarves or other coverings, some Islamic countries insist that all women must cover up, no matter what faith the woman follows. In the United States, students can wear headscarves or other religious symbols to public schools because these symbols are considered an expression of faith, which is protected by the First Amendment.

On the other hand, a teacher wearing a headscarf in a public school would be seen as representing the government. Wearing a headscarf or any prominent religious symbol would identify a teacher with one religion.

Crosses and Headscarves

In 1895, the state of Pennsylvania passed the Garb Statute, which said that religious clothing was not appropriate for a governmental representative. That law was not challenged until 1990, when a Muslim teacher, Alima Delores Reardon, wanted to wear a headscarf to the Philadelphia school she taught in. Despite the Garb Statute, for many years, teachers had worn religious jewelry such as crosses and the Star of David with no comment.[5]

The Third U.S. Circuit Court of Appeals upheld the state

law and said the teacher couldn't dress in a way that associated her with any one religion because "the preservation of religious neutrality [in public schools] is a compelling state interest."[6]

This case was cited in 2003 when a teacher's aide named Brenda Nichols was suspended from a school in Pittsburgh, Pennsylvania, because she wore a 1¼-inch cross to the classroom in which she worked. U.S. District Judge Arthur Schwab said the law did not apply to Nichols because she was an uncertified teacher's aide. He said Nichols should be reinstated and given back pay because the school's policy was "openly and overtly averse to religion."[7]

> In the United States, students can wear headscarves or other religious symbols to public schools because these symbols are considered an expression of faith, which is protected by the First Amendment.

"A Teacher's Guide to Religion in Public Schools," written by seventeen religious and educational organizations, suggests that teachers can wear jewelry with religious symbolism as long as it is not very noticeable. For example, a teacher can wear a small cross or Star of David because that would be expressing his or her faith, but not a T-shirt that says "Jesus Saves," because that would be preaching.[8]

Pentacles and Pentagrams

What about Wicca, which some people say is one of the fastest growing religions in the United States?[9] In 2002, a high school freshman named Rebecca Moreno was suspended for wearing pentacle jewelry, which symbolizes her family's Wiccan beliefs. The pentacle is a five-pointed star inside a circle.

Officials at the North Texas high school said Moreno could come back to school if she wore the pentacle inside her clothing. Moreno said that the pentacle is an important symbol in her religion and wearing it in full view is her First Amendment

Wiccans celebrate the holiday of Samhain, the new year, by lighting candles. Many practitioners of Wicca say they have experienced discrimination.

right. School officials said they did not ban the symbol on religious grounds but because it was disruptive. Eventually the school decided she could wear the necklace as long as it did not disrupt the school.

"We just want the religious freedom that everybody else does," said Moreno.[10]

Occasionally, religious statements in dress and grooming conflict with workplace requirements. For example, in 1999, two Muslim police officers wanted to grow beards, even though the Newark Police Department that employed them had ruled that the only reason for not doing so was when shaving caused extreme skin irritation.

The Third United States Court of Appeals in Philadelphia ruled that Muslim police officers could grow beards while working. Allowing the Muslim officers the chance to express themselves through their grooming was an important part of their right to freely express their faith.[11]

While Muslim women are free to cover their faces, doing so can present a legal disadvantage or problem. A Florida judge ruled that a woman who covered her face with a veil could not get a driver's license.[12]

Circuit Judge Janet C. Thorpe said that although the woman held a sincere religious belief that she should wear the hijab in front of all strangers, the requirement that she have a photo taken by a female officer in a private room did not burden her right to the free exercise of religion. Having access to photo identification helps the police protect the public.[13]

Rules about what you can wear on your head while taking your driver's license photo vary from state to state, but no states allow you to cover your face, whatever your religious belief. So far, forty-six states have passed laws or enacted policies addressing the religious needs of people who wear head coverings.

Religious Symbols in the Workplace

There are many ways to dress or groom your hair that are considered an expression of faith. They include:

- **Muslim men growing a beard to honor the prophet Muhammad.**
- **Buddhist monks and nuns shaving their heads to show humility.**
- **Sikh men and women never cutting their hair and men wearing it up under a turban.**
- **Orthodox Jewish women covering their hair with a wig or scarf when around men to whom they are not related.**

Georgia, Kansas, Kentucky, and New Hampshire have no laws about head coverings in driver's license photos.[14]

Some states are working to find compromises, acceptable to women who want to cover their faces because of religious beliefs. In Michigan's state DMV offices, for example, arrangements are made to let women who normally wear face veils have their photographs taken privately. Headscarves are permitted, just not veils that cover the face.

Many American Muslim women choose to wear the hijab, or headscarf, as a sign of their faith.

"If they asked me to take off my scarf, I would be angry. I'd make a scene," said sixteen-year-old Huda Mahmud of Dearborn, Michigan. "My scarf is part of me." Mahmud does not usually wear a face veil, but some of her friends who wear veils remove them for driver's license photographs.[15]

Deciding to cover your face could also affect how you are treated in a courtroom. A judge in Michigan dismissed the court case filed by a Muslim woman because she would not remove her veil when she testified. Judge Paul Paruk said he needed to see the woman's face to decide if she was telling the truth.

"I didn't feel like the court recognized me as a person that needed justice," said Ginnah Muhammad, who filed a complaint against the judge.[16]

Tolerance and T-shirts

What if you strongly support your religion's views on a subject the school wants to promote tolerance for? Can you wear a T-shirt that expresses your views, and is wearing that T-shirt your right under the Free Exercise Clause?

Tyler Chase Harper, sixteen, did not agree with his school's message of tolerance toward homosexuality. So one day, in 2004, he wore a T-shirt to school, expressing his view that "homosexuality is shameful."

"I presented a message that was scriptural, biblical," said Harper, who wore the T-shirt with the antigay message on the annual Day of Silence. The Day of Silence is held in high schools and colleges to recognize discrimination against gay, lesbian, bisexual, and transgender students and to promote tolerance.

The first time Harper wore an antigay T-shirt, the Poway, California, school did nothing. However, the next day he wore another shirt with the additional message, "Be Ashamed." A teacher asked him to remove the shirt, saying it was against the school's dress code. That code says that students may not wear any clothing that promotes or portrays "violence or hate behavior, including derogatory connotations toward sexual identity."

Harper refused and was suspended. He and his family sued the school district, saying that his free speech rights had been violated.[17]

The U.S. Court of Appeals for the Ninth Circuit Court did not agree that Harper had a right to wear the T-shirt without school interference. They did not agree that this action fell under the Free Exercise Clause, because it reflected his religious belief. The court concluded that school officials only needed to show a rational reason for their actions, which in this case were explained by the school's dress code.[18]

Symbols on the Wall

Religious symbols can be clothes, jewelry, or what you use to decorate a building. Words or images placed on the walls of schools and government buildings can give the impression that the institution favors one religion. What would you think about a school that hung a painting of Jesus right next to the principal's office? Would it matter if you were not Christian? How would you feel about the justice doled out in a court that prominently displayed the Ten Commandments? Would you be afraid that it would favor some over others?

When attorney Harold Sklar moved to Bridgeport, West Virginia, in the late 1990s, and enrolled his children in the high school, he was amazed to discover a large portrait of Jesus hanging outside the principal's office. In the schools he attended growing up, hall portraits included George Washington and Abraham Lincoln. Because he was Jewish, the picture made him feel very uncomfortable. Displaying Jesus seemed to say that one religion was favored in the school. Being an attorney with the U.S. Justice Department, he knew that it was probably unconstitutional.

After a decade of asking the school to take the picture down and being ignored, Sklar and a teacher at the school, Jacqueline McKenzie, filed a lawsuit in 2006, with the support of the organization Americans United for Separation of Church and State and the ACLU of West Virginia. The lawsuit was known as *Sklar* v. *Board of Education.* Sklar was sure he could win his case because a 1993 case, *Washegesic* v. *Bloomingdale* had ruled a similar picture to be unconstitutional.

Officials at the school refused to remove the picture and called the lawsuit grounds for "an all-out war."[19] In August of 2006, thirty-seven years after the picture was hung on the wall, it was stolen. Instead of dropping the case, the community hoped to replace the painting.

"I know our community," said Pattae Kinney, a parent of

This painting of Jesus in the hall of Bridgeport High School was stolen after a lawsuit was filed to have it removed.

one of the school's students. "And we're very in favor of keeping this painting."[20]

In September, the picture was replaced with a mirror donated by the Christian Freedom Alliance; an inscription on the mirror mentioned Jesus Christ. On legal advice, the school removed the inscription. Americans United for Separation of Church and State agreed to withdraw the suit if the school did not replace the painting with another religious article.[21]

The Ten Commandments

Many government buildings, parks, and courts display the Ten Commandments. The commandments are part of the heritage of Christianity, Judaism, and Islam, yet each interprets the commandments differently. Even within Christianity, various denominations interpret them differently. Some religious leaders feel that the commandments serve as an example of moral behavior and should be included in schools, courthouses, and other public buildings.

"The problems we face in America are moral problems, which cannot be solved legislatively or judicially. We need a moral code to address them," said Robert Schenck, founder of the National Clergy Council. "There is no better educational or moral code than the Ten Commandments."[22]

Other people say the commandments should be displayed in courthouses because they serve as the basis of the nation's laws. While there may or may not be merit to displaying the Ten Commandments, the courts have concerned themselves with whether such cases are constitutional.

In 1980, Sydell Stone and other parents whose children attended a Kentucky school challenged a Kentucky state law that required the posting of the Ten Commandments in each public school classroom. The Supreme Court ruled 5–4 that this violated the Establishment Clause because posting them was "religious in nature." The court also said the commandments were not limited to secular matters such as murder and stealing, but talked about religious matters such as the worship of God.[23]

Although many judges have ruled against displaying the Ten Commandments, one judge felt that displaying them was so important, it cost him his job. In 1992, Judge Roy Moore placed a plaque with the Ten Commandments in his Gadsden, Alabama, courtroom. In 1997, a federal judge asked him to remove it, which Moore refused to do. Moore ran for chief justice of the Alabama Supreme Court as the "10 Commandments judge." He had a two-ton granite monument to the commandments built in his court in 2001, was ordered

A monument showing the Ten Commandments is removed from outside an Ohio high school, following the ruling of a federal judge. The Supreme Court has ruled that many such displays violate the Establishment Clause.

to remove it, and again refused. In 2003, a judicial ethics panel removed him from office, saying he had put himself above the law.

"It's not about a monument," said Moore. "It's not about religion. It's about acknowledgment of almighty God."[24]

Workers removed the monument in 2003. While Moore and his supporters felt the Ten Commandments were the foundation of the nation's legal system and that forbidding the acknowledgment of God violates the free expression of religion, a lawsuit filed against its installation said the marker endorsed Christianity.[25]

In 2003, Alabama's judicial ethics panel removed Justice Moore from office for violating a federal judge's order. The panel said he put himself above the law by "willfully and publicly" flouting the order to remove the monument.[26]

When the Commandments Are Appropriate

There have been seemingly contradictory court rulings on whether or not the Ten Commandments can be displayed. The contradiction may have something to do with whether the commandments are viewed as being purely religious symbols or as part of the nation's legal heritage. The finer points of this argument may yet be open to debate.

In 2005, Thomas Van Orden sued Texas because he said that displaying the Ten Commandments at the state capitol meant that the state endorsed religion and violated the Establishment Clause. In *Van Orden* v. *Perry*, the Supreme Court ruled against Van Orden 5–4, saying that the commandments served a secular purpose, and a reasonable person would not think them an endorsement of religion. Though the Ten Commandments are religious, said Chief Justice William H. Rehnquist, "simply having religious content or promoting a message consistent with a religious doctrine does not run afoul of the establishment clause."[27]

That same year, the ACLU sued three Kentucky courthouses in federal district court for displaying framed versions of the Ten Commandments. The ACLU argued that these displays violated the Establishment Clause. The district court and Sixth Court of Appeals agreed. Justice David Souter said the displays violated the Establishment Clause because their purpose was to advance religion. One display of the commandments was displayed alone, one was displayed with texts of another religion, and the third was displayed with patriotic and political documents from American, colonial, and British history.[28]

Another court ruled that it is legal to include the commandments as part of a larger display. In August 2006, Judge Ronald A. White of Federal District Court in Muskogee, Oklahoma, said a Ten Commandments monument outside a courthouse could stay, rejecting arguments that it promotes Christianity over other religions. He found that the officials who created the display, which also recognizes war veterans, the Choctaw Tribe, and the Mayflower Compact, did not "overstep the constitutional line demarcating government neutrality toward religion."[29]

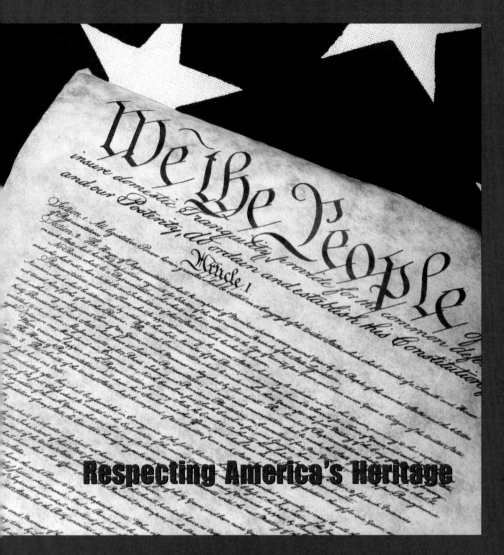

Respecting America's Heritage

Most Americans support the First Amendment and the freedoms it guarantees, but many are unsure how to interpret these freedoms in light of new developments.[1] The drafters of the Constitution could not have imagined many of today's controversies. For example, the Founding Fathers did not have to consider whether to teach a biblical explanation as an alternative to teaching about evolution in school. Science had not yet come up with an explanation that differed from the creation story found in the Bible.

When the Constitution was written, America was not as religiously diverse as it is today. For most of its history, the nation has been predominantly Protestant, making it somewhat easier to arrive at a general agreement of what was socially acceptable.

The majority may soon be history. According to the National Opinion Research Center's General Social Survey of 2004, the number of Protestants soon will slip below 50 percent of the nation's population. Less than 77 percent of Americans identify themselves as Christian, which is a significant decline from the less than 87 percent who considered themselves Christian in 1990.[2]

As the country becomes more diverse, some Americans may feel that their values no longer play as large a role in shaping the nation. This may be very difficult to accept and cause them to feel discriminated against. However, many people believe that the only way to respect any religion is to respect all religions.

According to First Amendment scholar Charles Haynes:

> This debate about how to get First Amendment rights in school won't go very deep and far until we step back and say, "How are we going to deal with the fact that there are 10 million ways of understanding the world, and how are we going to help students understand the 10 million ways? Or are we only going to allow one way, one lens for seeing all the subjects? This is the greatest challenge we have.[3]

Activists or Interpreters?

Democracy is a process. It is not fixed. It grows and reinterprets itself. Laws are passed. Laws are administered. Laws are challenged. Laws are reviewed. Laws stand up to judicial review and are ruled on. Laws are established for the good of all, but laws may not be considered to be good by all.

Some Americans feel that their country's moral foundation is being weakened by the rulings of the Supreme Court. Some judges who have made such controversial rulings as those on school prayer have been called activists. Some people say these judges are rewriting laws that people really want by deciding they are not constitutional.

The courts are part of the nation's system of checks and balances. The United States government has three branches—executive, legislative, and judicial. A system of checks and balances keeps any one branch from having too much power. The legislative branch makes a law, the executive branch signs or vetoes it and enforces it, and the judicial branch decides whether it is constitutional. Laws usually reach the courts because someone objects to them. Hearing a case provides a chance for the government to learn how a law affects the people it governs.

> As the country becomes more diverse, some Americans may feel that their values no longer play as large a role in shaping the nation. This may cause them to feel discriminated against.

While judges are influenced by their own beliefs and are appointed by people whose values they share, they must rule according to the test of constitutionality—as they interpret it. As you can see from reading any Supreme Court ruling, the Constitution is open to widely different interpretations.

Schools as a Civil Arena

Much religious debate has taken place about schools. To find common ground, it may help if people think of schools as a place where people of different religious faiths—and people of no faith—can interact and share their beliefs without any one religion being endorsed. The nation's public schools are not religious—but neither do they have to be religion-free.

In 2000, the Department of Education sent schools guidelines on how to develop religious liberty policies. It is hoped that if schools create policies and distribute them, any disputes over the religious rights of teachers and students can be resolved more quickly and more easily.[4]

For example, the Davis County School District in Utah

What Students Can Do

- It's okay to discuss religion and First Amendment rights with someone of a different religion or no religion at all, as long as you do so with respect and work toward a common ground.

- If you feel that your rights to express your religion have been denied, talk to a teacher, your parents, or an organization that can help protect your rights. Sometimes just talking to a teacher about an uncomfortable situation can help make changes.

- The same advice applies if you feel that you are being forced to participate in a religious exercise and it makes you feel uncomfortable. Talk to your teacher, your parents, or an organization that can help you protect your rights.

- Learn more about different religions and what their beliefs are. It's easier to understand concerns if you know the history and practices of that faith.

- Try to imagine how you might feel if you were on either side of a religious rights trial. Or if you were a judge ruling on these cases, what would you decide?

- Ask your school to create and distribute their policies on religious liberty and exercise.

sends out guidelines that detail exactly what is permitted for teachers and students. The guidelines promote an attitude of respect, outline what could be considered harassment, and offer a process in which problems can be resolved.[5]

Trespassing on the Rights of Others

When it comes to religious freedom, the rights of all citizens are only as strong as the rights of each citizen. The Pledge of Allegiance underscores the importance of "justice for all"—not for one group or even the majority, but justice for all. Justice for all can be a tall order, but many believe it is exactly that effort that makes the nation great.

According to Diana L. Ecka, a professor of comparative religion:

> As the new century dawns, we Americans are challenged to make good on the promise of religious freedom so basic to the very idea and image of America. Religious freedom has always given rise to religious diversity, and never has our diversity been more dramatic than it is today. This will require us to reclaim the deepest meaning of the very principles we cherish and to create a truly pluralist American society in which this great diversity is not simply tolerated but becomes the very source of our strength. But to do this, we will all need to know more than we do about one another and to listen for the new ways in which new Americans articulate the "we" and contribute to the sound and spirit of America.[6]

When the Constitution was written, the Founding Fathers knew that applying its principles would sometimes pose a challenge. In a letter in 1832, James Madison, known as Father of the Constitution, acknowledged that it could be difficult to know how to apply the Constitution, especially when it came to the separation of church and state. He wrote: "It may not be easy, in every possible case, to trace the separation between the rights of religion and the civil authority with such distinctions as to avoid collisions and doubts on unessential points."

Madison said the only way to preserve the peace would be for the government to stay out of the dispute, unless it meant preserving the peace, and to protect each sect from trespassing on the rights of others.[7]

Chapter Notes

Chapter 1 Religion and Public Life

1. Lindsay Layton, "Pitting Law Against God," *The Washington Post*, June 22, 1999, <Washingtonpost.com/wpsrv/style/features/becker062299.htm> (September 1, 2006).

2. David L. Hudson, "Pledge of Allegiance Overview," First Amendment Center, n.d., <http://www.firstamendmentcenter.org/speech/studentexpression/topic.aspx?topic=pledge> (September 21, 2006).

3. "Court Decisions on Prayers During Graduation Ceremonies at U.S. Public Schools," ReligiousTolerance.org, n.d., <http://www.religioustolerance.org/ps_prae.htm> (September 21, 2006).

4. Layton.

5. "Federal Appeals Panel Sides With Student Bible Club Leader," Freedomforum.org, September 10, 2002, <http://www.freedomforum.org/templates/document.asp?documentID=16932> (September 2, 2006).

6. Benjamin Dowling-Sendor, "A Question of Equality," *American School Board Journal*, February 2003, vol. 190, no. 2, <http://www.asbsj.com/2003/02/0203schoollaw.html> (September 2, 2006).

7. "Federal Appeals Panel Sides With Student Bible Club Leader."

8. "Christmas censored in Jackson County, Georgia?" Alliance Defense Fund, November 29, 2005, <http://www.alliancedefensefund.org/news/story.aspx?cid=3607> (August 18, 2006).

9. "ACLU of Rhode Island Sues on Behalf of Town Resident's Objections to City Hall Religious Display," ACLU Web site, December 22, 2003, <http://www.aclu.org/religion/gen/16093prs20031222.html> (August 18, 2006).

10. Ibid.

11. "Law of the Land: ACLU loses Christmas Case," *Worldnetdaily.com*, November 16, 2004, <http://www.worldnetdaily.com/news/article.asp?ARTICLE_ID=41469> (August 18, 2006).

12. "Is the ACLU Anti-Religion?" ACLU ProCon.org, n.d., <http://www.acluprocon.org/bin/procon/procon.cgi?database=5-E-Sub1Q.db&command=viewone&op=t&id=2&rnd=946.9036398435271> (August 20, 2006).

13. Kimberly Winston, "The Christmas Tipping Point," Beliefnet.com, n.d., <http://www.beliefnet.com/story/158/story_15819_1.html> (August 18, 2006).

14. Ibid.

15. Terry Frieden, "U.S. to Defend Muslim Girl Wearing Scarf in School," CNN.com, March 31, 2004, <www.cnn.com/2004/law/03/30/us.school.headcarves/index.html?iref=newssearch> (August 20, 2006).

16. Maura Farrelly, "Oklahoma School Bans Student From Wearing Religious Attire," *The Epoch Times*, April 14, 2004, <http://en.epochtimes.com/news/4-4-14/20913.html> (August 31, 2006).

17. "Justice Department Reaches Settlement Agreement With Oklahoma School District in Muslim Student Headscarf Case," U.S. Department of Justice, press release, May 19, 2004, <http://www.usdoj.gov/opa/pr/2004/May/04_crt_343.htm> (August 31, 2006).

18. Farrelly.

19. "Overview of the Ten Commandments Debate," Religious Tolerance.org, n.d., <http://www.religioustolerance.org/chr_10ci.htm> (September 2, 2006).

20. Associated Press, "Ten Commandments Plaque Ordered Out of Pennsylvania Courthouse," Freedomforum.org, March 7, 2002, <http://www.freedomforum.org/templates/document.asp?documentID=15834> (August 20, 2006).

21. "Help Us to Support Freedom of Speech and Prevent Discrimination," Summum Web site, n.d., <http://www.summum.us/about/freespeech.shtml> (July 13, 2007).

22. *Summum* v. *Ogden*, 10CIR 795, 01-4022 (2002).

23. "Utah Decalogs Moved," Freedom From Religion Foundation, *Freethought Today*, vol. 20, no. 6, August 2003, <http://ffrf.org/fttoday/2003/aug/index.php?ft=statechurch> (July 13, 2007).

24. "Maryland Teen Questions Commandments Monument in City Park," Freedomforum.org, May 16, 2002, <http://www.freedom forum.org/templates/document.asp?documentID=16260> (August 20, 2006).

25. Brent Nicastro, "Thou Shalt Defend Thy First Amendment," Freedom From Religion Foundation, *Freethought Today*, vol. 20, no. 1, January/February 2003, <http://www.ffrf.org/fttoday/2003/janfeb/index.php?ft=trettien> (September 2, 2006).

26. Ibid.

Chapter 2 Faith of the Founding Fathers

1. Jon Meacham, *American Gospel: God, the Founding Fathers, and the Making of a Nation* (New York: Random House, 2006), p. 55.

2. Frank Lambert, *The Founding Fathers and the Place of Religion in America* (Princeton, N.J.: Princeton University Press, 2003), p. 17.

3. Meacham, p. 49.

4. Ibid., p. 58.

5. David L. Holmes, *The Faiths of the Founding Fathers* (New York: Oxford University Press, 2006), p. 5.

6. Meacham, pp. 54–55.

7. Ibid., p. 8.

8. "Is America a Christian Nation?" pamphlet, Americans United for Separation of Church and State, Washington, D.C., n.d., pp. 2–3.

9. Holmes, p. 88.

10. "Jefferson's Letter to the Danbury Baptists," Library of Congress information bulletin, June 1998, vol. 57, no. 6, <www.loc.gov/loc/lcib/9806/danpost.html> (September 21, 2006).

11. W. W. Hening, ed., *Statutes at Large of Virginia*, vol. 12 (1823), pp. 84–86.

12. "The First Amendment to the U.S. Constitution: Religious Aspects," ReligiousTolerance.org, n.d., <http://www.religious tolerance.org/amend_1.htm> (September 17, 2006).

13. James Hutson, "James Madison and the Social Utility of Religion:

Risks vs. Rewards," Library of Congress, n.d., <http://www.loc. gov/loc/madison/hutson-paper.html> (September 17, 2006).

14. Ibid.

15. Lambert, p. 239.

16. Don Erler, "Of Polygamy and Privacy," *Fort Worth Star Telegram*, Startelegram.com, April 4, 2006, <http://www.dfw.com/mld/ dfw/news/opinion/14258836.htm> (September 17, 2006).

17. *Cantwell* v. *Connecticut*, 310 U.S. 296 (1940); see also Oyez U.S. Supreme Court Multimedia, "*Cantwell* v. *Connecticut*," n.d., <http://www.oyez.org/oyez/resource/case/65/print> (September 22, 2006); "First Amendment Topics: Cantwell v. Connecticut," First Amendment Center, n.d., <http://www.firstamendmentcenter. org/faclibrary/case.aspx?case=Cantwell_v_CT> (September 22, 2006).

18. *McCollum* v. *Board of Education, School District 71*, 1948, 333 U.S. 203.

19. "Vashti McCollum, Brought Landmark Church-State Suit," *The Cleveland Plain Dealer*, August 27, 2006, <http://www.cleveland. com/news/plaindealer/index.ssf?/base/news/115666792255560.xm l&coll=2> (September 24, 2006).

20. *McCollum* v. *Board of Education, School District 71*.

21. *Zorach* v. *Clauson*, 343 U.S. 306.

22. Ibid.

23. *Everson* v. *Ewing*, 330 U.S. 1.

Chapter 3 Prayer

1. "Only a Teacher: Horace Mann," PBS.org, n.d., <http://www.pbs. org/onlyateacher/horace.html> (September 22, 2006).

2. "Introduction to the *Engel* v. *Vitale* Court Case," United States Information Agency, n.d., <http://usinfo.state.gov/usa/infousa/ facts/democrac/47.htm> (September 22, 2006).

3. David L. Hudson, Jr., "Plaintiff in 1962 School-Prayer Case Reflects On His Role," First Amendment Center, August 26,

2006, <http://www.firstamendmentcenter.org/analysis.aspx?id=
15701> (September 25, 2006).

4. Ibid.

5. George DeWan, "School Prayer Divides LI," *Newsday Community Guide*, Long Island History, n.d., <http://www.newsday.com/
community/guide/lihistory/ny-history-hs817a,0,7813062.story>
(September 25, 2006).

6. "School Prayer," First Amendment Center Web site, n.d., <http://
www.firstamendmentcenter.org/rel_liberty/publicschools/topic.asp
x?topic=school_prayer> (September 25, 2006).

7. Hudson.

8. DeWan.

9. Caitlin Johnson, "School Prayer Then and Now," Connect for Kids
Web site, June 26, 2000, <http://www.connectforkids.org/node/
205> (October 1, 2006).

10. "Freethinker of the Year," Freedom from Religion Foundation Web
site, n.d., <http://www.ffrf.org/awards/ftoy/> (September 25, 2006).

11. *Wallace* v. *Jaffree*, 472 U.S. 38 (1985).

12. David L. Hudson, Jr., "African-American First Amendment
Heroes," First Amendment Center, February 20, 2004,
<http://www.firstamendmentcenter.org/analysis.aspx?id=12734>
(July 13, 2007).

13. *Lee* v. *Weisman*, 505 US 577 (1992).

14. *Lemon* v. *Kurtzman*, 403 US 602 (1971).

15. *Santa Fe Independent School Dist.* v. *Doe*, 530 U.S. 290 (2000).

16. "Guidance on Constitutionally Protected Prayer in Public
Elementary and Secondary Schools," U.S. Department of
Education, February 7, 2003, <http://www.ed.gov/policy/gen/
guid/religionandschools/prayer_guidance.html> (September 26,
2006).

17. Michelle Goldberg, "How the Secular Humanist Grinch Didn't
Steal Christmas," Salon.com, November 21, 2005, <http://
dir.salon.com/story/news/feature/2005/11/21/christmas/index.html?
pn=3> (August 19, 2006).

18. "See You at the Pole: September 26, 2007," See You at the Pole Web site, n.d., <http://www.syatp.com/home/index.html> (October 25, 2007).

19. Karen Heinselman, "Students Take Faith Public," *Waterloo-Cedar Falls Courier*, June 8, 2006, <http://www.wcfcourier.com/articles/2006/06/08/news/top_story/a146feccf43e44638625718700475b56.txt> (September 26, 2006).

20. William J. Murray, *Let Us Pray: A Plea for Prayer in Our Schools* (New York: William Morrow and Company,1995), p. 197.

21. "Jewish Family Flees Delaware School District's Aggressive Christianity," Jews On First Web site, June 28, 2006, <http://www.jewsonfirst.org/06b/indianriver.html> (September 26, 2006).

22. Ibid.

23. Richard J. Ellis, *To the Flag* (Lawrence, Kans.: University Press of Kansas, 2005), pp. 85–86.

24. Ibid., p. 2.

25. "A Matter of Conscience," American Treasures of Library of Congress, letter within the article by William Gobitas, n.d., <http://www.loc.gov/exhibits/treasures/trr006.html> (September 24, 2006).

26. "Freedom of Speech and Religion: Bill Gobitas," The Bill of Rights Institute, n.d., <http://www.billofrightsinstitute.org/Instructional/Resources/Lessons/Lessons_List.asp?action=showDetails&id=109&ref=showCatD&catId=8> (September 24, 2006).

27. *West Virginia Board of Education* v. *Barnett*, 319 U.S. 624.

28. Ellis, p. 108.

29. Ibid., p. 106.

30. West Virginia Board of Education v. Barnett.

31. Peter N. Herndon, "In God We Trust: Public Schools and Religious Freedom," Yale-New Haven Teachers Institute, March 1, 2003, <www.yale.edu/ynhti/curriculum/units/2004/1/04.01.03.x.html> (September 22, 2006).

32. Robert Longley, "Brief History of the Pledge of Allegiance," United

States Information Agency, n.d., <http://usgovinfo.about.com/cs/usconstitution/a/pledgehist.htm> (September 25, 2006).

33. "Atheist Father Cannot Sue Over Use of 'Under God,'" CNN.com, June 15, 2004, <http://www.cnn.com/2004/LAW/06/14/scotus.pledge/> (September 25, 2006).

34. "High Court: Atheist Can't Challenge 'God' in Pledge," First Amendment Center, June 14, 2004, <http://www.firstamendmentcenter.org/news.aspx?id=13519> (September 25, 2006).

35. "Poll: Keep 'Under God' in Pledge of Allegiance," March 24, 2004, First Amendment Center Web site, <http://www.firstamendmentcenter.org/news.aspx?id=12989> (October 24, 2007).

Chapter 4 Religion in School

1. Charles Haynes, "Finding Common Ground," Freedomforum.org, n.d., p. 73, <http://www.freedomforum.org/templates/document.asp?documentID=3979> (October 1, 2006).

2. Ibid., pp. 74–83.

3. "The Philadelphia Riots of 1844," The Historical Society of Pennsylvania, n.d., <http://www.hsp.org/files/studentreadingriotsinthecityofbrotherlylove.pdf> (October 1, 2006).

4. *Abington* v. *Schempp*, 374 U.S. 203 (1963).

5. William J. Murray, *Let Us Pray: A Plea for Prayer in Our Schools* (New York: William Morrow and Company, 1995), p. 12.

6. Ibid., pp. 16–19.

7. Ibid., p. 50.

8. Ibid., p. 196.

9. Ibid., p. xii.

10. *Abington* v. *Schempp*.

11. "The Bible and Public Schools," pamphlet, First Amendment Center, Nashville, Tenn., 1999, p. 2.

12. Charles C. Haynes, "Texas Bible Courses: Turning Public School Into the Local Church," First Amendment Center, September 17, 2006, <http://www.firstamendmentcenter.org/commentary.aspx?id=1390> (September 26, 2006).

13. Ibid.

14. Richard W. Riley, "Religious Expression in Public Schools," Department of Education, May 30, 1998, <http://www.ed.gov/Speeches/08-1995/religion.html> (September 27, 2006).

15. Ibid.

16. Marjorie Coeyman, "Religion-Free Zone?" *The Christian Science Monitor*, May 20, 2003, <http://www.csmonitor.com/2003/0520/p11s01-lepr.html> (July 16, 2007).

17. Amanda Paulson, "When Is Religion Okay in School?" CBS News, January 27, 2005, <http://www.cbsnews.com/stories/2005/01/31/national/main670346.shtml> (July 21, 2007).

18. *Hedges* v. *Wauconda Community School District*, 118, 9 F.3d 1295, 1298 (7th Cir., 1993).

19. *Hills* v. *Scottsdale Unified School District*, No. 48, 329 F.3d 1044 (9th Cir., 2003); see also "High Court Won't Review Religious-fliers Case," First Amendment Center, January 21, 2004, <http://www.firstamendmentcenter.org/news.aspx?id=12488> (October 25, 2007).

20. USC 4071, Title 20, Education, Chapter 52, Education for Economic Security, Subchapter VIII, Equal Access, Department of Justice, n.d., <http://www.usdoj.gov/crt/cor/byagency/ed4071.htm> (July 22, 2007).

21. Ibid.

22. Ibid.

23. Ibid.

24. *Westside Community Board of Education* v. *Mergens*, 496 U.S. 226 (1990).

25. Benjamin Dowling-Sendor, "A Case of Free Speech Rights," *American School Board Journal*, August 2001, vol. 188, no. 9, <http://www.asbj.com/2001/09/0901schoollaw> (September 26, 2006).

26. "Supreme Court Collection: *Good News Club* v. *Milford Central School* (99-2036), 533 U.S. 98 (2001)," Cornell University Law School, n.d., <http://supct.law.cornell.edu/supct/html/99-2036.ZS.html> (June 19, 2007).

27. Ibid.

28. "Religious Discrimination," The U.S. Equal Employment Opportunity Commission, n.d., <http://www.eeoc.gov/types/religion.html> (September 30, 2006).

29. *Wisconsin* v. *Yoder*, 06 U.S. 205 (1972).

30. "School Violence Helps Spur Rise in Home Schooling," CNN.com, August 17, 1999, <www.cnn.com/US/9908/17/home.schooling> (July 21, 2007).

31. John Stossel, Sylvia Johnson, and Lynn Redmond, "The Black Sheep of Hardesty," ABC News, May 11, 2007, <http://abcnews.go.com/2020/story?id=3164811&page=1> (July 21, 2007).

32. *Smalkowski* v. *Hardesty Public School District*, No. CIV-06-845-M (2006).

33. Stossel, Johnson, and Redmond.

Chapter 5 Holiday Celebrations

1. Patrik Jonsson, "Banned at the schoolhouse door: pint-size ghosts and goblins," *The Christian Science Monitor*, October 31, 2005, <www.csmonitor.com/2005/1031/p02s01-ussc.html> (October 5, 2006).

2. Mark J. Friedman, "Specter of Empty Chairs Haunts Hebrew Schools on Halloween," *The Jewish News Weekly*, October 31, 1997, <www.jewishsf.com/content/2-0-/module/displaystory/> (October 5, 2006).

3. Jonsson.

4. "Christmas project," Alliance Defense Fund, n.d., <http://www.alliancedefensefund.org/issues/religiousfreedom/default.aspx?cid=3570> (October 3, 2006).

5. "Once Upon a Time, When Christmas Was Banned," *Massachusetts Travel Journal*, n.d., <http://www.masstraveljournal.com/features/1101chrisban> (September 29, 2006).

6. Adam Cohen, "This Season's War Cry: Commercialize Christmas or Else," *The New York Times*, December 4, 2005, <http://www.nytimes.com/2005/12/04/opinion/04sun3.html?ex=1291352400&en=a1c102d8260b92e3&ei=5088&partner=rssnyt&emc=rss> (September 29, 2006).

7. Stephen Nissenbaum, *The Battle for Christmas* (New York: Vintage, 1997), pp. 195–196.

8. Laura Schiavo, "1923 National Christmas Tree," National Park Service, U.S. Department of the Interior, n.d., <http://www.nps.gov/whho/historyculture/1923-national-christmas-tree.htm> (October 4, 2006).

9. Cohen.

10. Jonathan Chisdes, "On Being a Minority in America," *L'Chaim*, November 1999, <http://www.chisdes.com/minority.html> (October 4, 2006).

11. "Who is St. Nicholas?" n.d., <http://www.stnicholascenter.org/Brix?pageID=38> (October 4, 2006).

12. Ignazio Messina, "Schools Lean to 'Holiday Trees' As Spirit of Inclusiveness Grows," *Toledo Blade*, December 3, 2005, <http://toledoblade.com/apps/pbcs.dll/article?AID=/20051203/NEWS04/512030379/0/NEWS28> (October 4, 2006).

13. John Gibson, *The War on Christmas* (New York: Sentinel HC, 2005), p. xxv.

14. Ibid., pp. 1–2, 5.

15. "Portraits of Ordinary Muslims: United States," PBS.org, n.d., <http://www.pbs.org/wgbh/pages/frontline/shows/muslims/portraits/us.html#facts> (October 4, 2006).

16. Daniel de Vise, "Floating holidays urged for schools," *The Washington Post*, December 25, 2004, <http://www.washingtonpost.com/wp-dyn/articles/A24989-2004Dec24.html> (October 4, 2006).

17. Joe Garafoli, "Falwell fighting for holy holiday," *San Francisco Chronicle*, November 20, 2005, p. A-1.

18. "Defending religious freedom," Alliance Defense Fund, n.d., <http://www.alliancedefensefund.org/issues/religiousfreedom/Default.aspx> (October 4, 2006).

19. "Conservative Christians say 'happy holidays' isn't good enough," First Amendment Center, December 18, 2004, <http://www.firstamendmentcenter.org/news.aspx?id=14565> (October 4, 2006).

20. *Lynch* v. *Donnelly*, 465 U.S. 668 (1984).

21. *Allegheny* v. *ACLU*, 492 U.S. 573 (1989).

22. "Oklahoma voters punish schools for Nativity removal," First Amendment Center, December 17, 2004, <http://www.firstamendmentcenter.org/news.aspx?id=14560> (October 4, 2006).

23. Bob Nigh, "Oklahoma School System Adopts Religious Liberty Protection Policy," *Baptist Press*, May 10, 2005, <http://www.bpnews.net/bpnews.asp?ID=20759> (July 16, 2007).

24. Ibid.

25. "ACLJ Files Federal Suit Against Oregon School Dist. After Student Prohibited From Distributing Christmas Card," American Center for Law and Justice, April 23, 2004, <http://www.aclj.org/News/Read.aspx?ID=383> (October 4, 2006).

26. Catherine Trevison, "Suit Settled Over Religious Cards at School," *The Oregonian*, October 20, 2004, <http://www.aclj.org/News/Read.aspx?ID=623> (July 16, 2007).

27. "Chapter 13: The Brownsville Public School Boycott: 1905," The American Jewish Historical Society, n.d., <www.ajhs.org/publications/chapters/chapter.cfm?documentID=198> (October 7, 2006).

28. Robert Wiener, "Carols out in New Jersey schools," *The Jewish Times*, December 1, 2004, <http://www.jewishtimes.com/scripts/edition.pl?now=5/25/1999&SubSectionID=31&ID=4363> (October 7, 2006).

29. "School's ban on Christmas carols sparks debate," MSNBC, December 22, 2004, <http://www.msnbc.msn.com/id/6745305/> (October 7, 2006).

30. Ralph Z. Hallow, "Carolers protest religious-music ban," *The Washington Times*, December 22, 2004, <http://washingtontimes. com/national/20041221-103610-9207r.htm> (October 7, 2006).

31. Jim Brown, "Lawsuit Challenges NJ Schools' Christmas Music Ban," Agape Press, December 27, 2004, <http://headlines.aga pepress.org/archive/12/272004b.asp> (October 9, 2006).

32. "Tis the Season for Disputes Over Holiday Observances," First Amendment Center, December 4, 2006, <http://www.firstamend mentcenter.org/news.aspx?id=17848> (July 16, 2007).

33. Charles Haynes, "Educating for Freedom and Responsibility," First Amendment Center, December 16, 2004, <http://www.firstamend mentschools.org/news/article.aspx?id=14558> (October 3, 2006).

34. "What Should Schools Do in December?" First Amendment Center, n.d., <http://www.firstamendmentschools.org/freedoms/ faq.aspx?id=12976> (October 3, 2006).

35. Haynes.

36. "Does December Spell Dilemma in Your School?" *Education World*, n.d., <http://www.education-world.com/a_curr/curr042.shtml> (October 3, 2006).

Chapter 6 Symbols of Faith

1. "French scarf ban comes into force," BBC News, September 2, 2004, <http://news.bbc.co.uk/1/hi/world/europe/3619988.stm> (October 9, 2006).

2. Daniel Williams, "In France, Students Observe Scarf Ban," *The Washington Post*, September 3, 2004, p. A-11.

3. Hannah Godfrey, "Schools' bid for headscarf ban widens French divide," *The Observer*, June 15, 2003, <http://observer.guardian. co.uk/islam/story/0,,977747,00.html> (October 9, 2006).

4. Williams.

5. "Veiled in Controversy" Religious Tolerance.org, n.d., <http://www.tolerance.org/teach/current/event.jsp?cid=271> (October 17, 2006).

6. "Teacher's Aide Suspended for Wearing Cross," TV station KDKA,

April 24, 2003, <http://kdka.com/local/local_story_114110626. html> (0ctober 17, 2006).

7. "Pennsylvania school agrees to retain cross-wearing teacher's aide," First Amendment Center, August 31, 2003, <http://www.first amendmentcenter.org/news.aspx?id=11875> (October 17, 2006).

8. A Teacher's Guide to Religion in Public Schools," Department of Education, n.d., <http://www.ed.gov/inits/religionandschools/ guides.html> (October 30, 2006).

9. "Religious Identification in the U.S.," Religious Tolerance.org, n.d., <http://www.religioustolerance.org/chr_prac2.htm> (October 21, 2006).

10. "Texas school superintendent allows Wiccan student to wear pentacle," First Amendment Center, September 12, 2002, <http://www.firstamendmentcenter.org/news.aspx?id=3446>; "Religious Clothing and Jewelry in School," Religious Tolerance. org, n.d., <http://www.religioustolerance.org/sch_clot5.htm> (October 10, 2006).

11. "In Brief: Appeals Panel Rules Officers in Newark Can Keep Beards," *The New York Times*, March 7, 1999, <http://query.ny times.com/gst/fullpage.html?res=9C0DE7D7173FF934A35750C0 A96F958260> (October 16, 2006).

12. "Judge: Woman Can't Cover Face on Driver's License," CNN.com, June 10, 2003, <http://www.cnn.com/2003/LAW/06/06/florida. license.veil/> (October 30, 2006).

13. Ibid.

14. "Religious Accommodation in Driver's License Photographs," Council on American-Islamic Relations, n.d., <www.islamiccenter lawrence.org/driversphoto.pdf> (July 20, 2007).

15. Ron French, "Michigan Tries to Accommodate Muslim Women," *The Detroit News*, June 11, 2003, <http://www.detnews.com/ 2003/metro/0306/11/e01-190059.htm> (July 21, 2007).

16. "Woman Who Won't Lift Veil Loses Lawsuit," ABC News, October 22, 2006, <abcnews.go.com/US/ wireStory?id=2598070& CMP=OTC-RSSFeeds0312> (October 23, 2006).

17. Blanca Gonzalez, "Student Sues Over Ban of Anti-Gay T-Shirt,"

Union Tribune, June 4, 2004, <http://www.signonsandiego.com/news/education/20040604-9999-1mi4powskul.html> (July 21, 2007).

18. National School Board Association, *Harper v. Poway Unified School District*, No. 04-57037 (9th Circuit), Legal Clips, April 2006, <http://www.nsba.org/site/doc_cosa.asp?TRACKID=&CID=487&DID=38413> (July 21, 2007).

19. Jeremy Leaming, "What's Wrong With This Picture?" Americans United for Separation of Church and State, n.d., <http://www.au.org/site/News2?page=NewsArticle&id=8504&news_iv_ctrl=0&abbr=cs_&JServSessionIdr010=fl7ip9pom1.app5b> (October 13, 2006).

20. "Negotiations continue: Town fights to keep Jesus Painting in school," MSNBC.com, August 20, 2006, <http://www.msnbc.msn.com/id/14443671/> (October 13, 2006).

21. "Inscription removed from Jesus Painting Replacement," *The Christian Post*, September 2, 2006, <www.christianpost.com/article/20060905/24265.htm> (October 13, 2006).

22. "The Ten Commandments (a.k.a. the Decalogue); Posting Them in Schools," Religious Tolerance.org, n.d., <http://www.religioustolerance.org/chr_10c1.htm> (October 13, 2006).

23. *Stone v. Graham*, 449 U.S. 39 (1980).

24. "The 10 Commandments Judge," PBS.org, n.d., <http://www.pbs.org/now/politics/roymoore.html> (October 17, 2006).

25. "Ten Commandments Monument Moved," CNN.com, November 14, 2003, <http://www.cnn.com/2003/LAW/08/27/ten.commandments/index.html> (October 21, 2006).

26. "Ten Commandments Judge Removed From Office," CNN.com, November 14, 2003, <http://www.cnn.com/2003/LAW/11/13/moore.tencommandments/> (July 21, 2007).

27. *Van Orden v. Perry*, 545 US 677 (2005).

28. *ACLU of Kentucky v. McCreary Courthouses*, No. 03-1693 (2005).

29. "Commandments Display Allowed," *The New York Times*, August 20, 2006, Section 1, p. 21.

Chapter 7 **Respecting America's Heritage**

1. Ken Paulson, "Time, healing bring renewed perspective on the First Amendment," First Amendment Center, August, 31, 2003, <http://www.firstamendmentcenter.org/commentary.aspx?id=11772> (November 24, 2006).

2. "Religious Identification in the U.S.: How American Adults View Themselves," ReligiousTolerance.org, n.d., <http://www.religious tolerance.org/chr_prac2.htm> (July 21, 2007).

3. Fielding Buck, "Religious liberty and public schools," FACSNET, November 4, 2002, <www.facsnet.org/issues/faith/haynes_pitts burgh.php> (November 22, 2004).

4. Charles Haynes, "Finding Common Ground," pp. 180, 181, Freedomforum.org, n.d., <http://www.freedomforum.org/ templates/document.asp?documentID=3979> (November 22, 2006).

5. Ibid., p. 178.

6. Diana L. Ecka, "A New Religious America," *Democracy*, November 2001, <http://usinfo.state.gov/journals/itdhr/1101/ijde/eck.htm> (July 21, 2007).

7. Lynda Beck Fenwick, *Should the Children Pray?* (Waco, Tex.: Markham Press Fund of Baylor University Press, 1989), p. 109.

Glossary

atheist—One who does not believe in or denies the existence of God or any supreme being.

banished—To be sent away from somewhere and forbidden to return.

circuit court—A U.S. federal trial court serving a judicial district. There are thirteen federal circuit courts of appeals.

civil—Applying to ordinary citizens, as in the terms *civil law* or *civil authority*. A civil court case is not the same as a criminal court case.

deism—An eighteenth-century religion that emphasized reason and not miracles.

heritage—Practices that are handed down from one generation to another.

Mehomitan—An old-fashioned way to describe Muslims, who follow Islam—the teachings of the prophet Muhammad.

Musselmen—Another old-fashioned way to describe Muslims.

nativist—One who favors native inhabitants over immigrants.

scrutiny—Close examination.

Socialist—A person who supports socialism, an economic system in which the government distributes the wealth so everyone has enough for basic needs.

Supreme Court—The highest court in the judicial branch of the U.S. government and the only one mentioned in the Constitution.

Further Reading

Haynes, Charles C., Sam Chaltain, and Susan M. Glisson. *First Freedoms: A Documentary History of First Amendment Rights in America.* Oxford, England: Oxford University Press, 2006.

Head, Tom, editor. *Religion and Education.* San Diego: Greenhaven Press, 2005.

Kowalski, Kathiann M. *Lemon* v. *Kurtzman and the Separation of Church and State Debate.* Berkeley Heights, N.J.: Enslow Publishers, Inc., 2005.

McIntosh, Kenneth R. and Marsha L. *Issues of Church, State and Religious Liberties: Whose Freedom, Whose Faith?* Philadelphia: Mason Crest Publishers, 2006.

Mountjoy, Shane. *Engel v. Vitale: School Prayer and the Establishment Clause.* New York: Chelsea House, 2006.

Zacharias, Gary, editor. *Freedom of Religion.* San Diego: Greenhaven Press, 2004.

Internet Addresses

Alliance Defense Fund
   \<http://www.alliancedefensefund.org\>

American Civil Liberties Union
   \<http://www.aclu.org\>

First Amendment Center
   \<http://www.firstamendmentcenter.org\>

Thomas More Law Center
   \<http://www.thomasmore.org\>

Index